WIRED *for* SUCCESS

The Leadership Journeys That Shaped Today's Top Technology Executives

First Edition: 2025

Published by:
Gifts Of Legacy LLC
Scottsdale, AZ 85255
Email: GiftsOfLegacy@gmail.com

ISBN: KDP Print - 978-1-968017-03-3
ISBN: KDP eBook - 978-1-968017-04-0
ISBN: KDP Hardcover - 978-1-968017-05-7
ISBN: Ingram Print - 978-1-968017-08-8
ISBN: Ingram Ebook - 978-1-968017-07-1

Library of Congress Control Number: 2025910031
Editing by: Elizabeth Paxton, ScratchCat LLC
Printed in the United States of America.

For information, bulk orders, or speaking engagements, please contact: GiftsOfLegacy@gmail.com

Table of Contents

Foreword

In the ever-evolving landscape of technology and business, the insights of those who have navigated its challenges are invaluable. This book, a collection of twenty essays penned by accomplished IT executives, offers a rare glimpse into the hard-earned lessons of leaders who have shaped the digital world.

Each chapter is a testament to resilience, innovation, and strategic foresight. As you read, you'll learn of the stories of Mary, Natalie, Denise, A Different Natalie, Dan, Kelly, Holliday, The Southern Gentleman, NeeCee, Kamal, Dorothy, Gary, Ed, The Father, Paula, Kevin, Monique, Kimberley, The Fool, Todd, Marline, Robert, Dallan, An Imaginary Spock, The Hero, Danira, Christine, Charles, and Sallie. They describe their successes, failures, insights, advice, strategies, mistakes, careers, tips, approaches to culture, politics, and even empathy. These stories are personal, insightful, and powerful.

It is a book of 20 journeys united in a focus on team (good and bad), leadership (inspired and not so much), management (or lack thereof), change (never just right but too fast, too slow, or not at all), people, ever-changing technology, lifelong learning—and ultimately, success in varying forms. I dare you to read this book and not recognize someone (or their doppelganger) you know.

As someone who has witnessed the transformative power of technology in business, I am honored to introduce this compendium. Whether you're an aspiring entrepreneur, a seasoned manager, or a professional charting your path in the corporate world, these stories and strategies will resonate. They distill decades of experience into practical wisdom, offering guidance on leadership, decision-making, and adapting to change.

This book is not just for IT professionals; it's for anyone in the business world eager to learn from those who have turned challenges into opportunities. I invite you to dive into these pages and discover the insights that will inspire and empower you on your own personal journey.

— Curtis A Carver Jr,
Vice President and CIO, UAB

Introduction to "Wired for Success"

Welcome to "Wired for Success," a compelling compilation of twenty chapters, each penned by expert IT executives who share their remarkable journeys through the ever-evolving world of information technology. These chapters are not just stories; they are powerful testimonies of resilience, innovation, and profound learning experiences that have shaped these leaders' careers and personal growth.

As members of the Info Tech Research Group executive book club, these IT executives come together regularly to exchange ideas, foster collaboration, and delve into the depths of leadership and technology. Their camaraderie extends beyond the book club meetings as they frequently participate in IT leadership events, where they continue to expand their horizons and influence the future of the industry.

In this book, you will find narratives that transcend mere professional achievements. Each chapter reveals the trials and triumphs faced by these leaders, offering a glimpse into the challenges of steering organizations through technological advancements, market dynamics, and organizational transformations.

From navigating complex projects to spearheading innovative solutions, the experiences shared in these pages are rich with insights and lessons learned. The impact of each experience is meticulously explored, providing readers with invaluable wisdom on adapting to change, fostering team spirit, and driving success in a fast-paced technology landscape.

Whether you are an aspiring IT professional, a seasoned executive, or simply someone interested in the world of technology leadership, "Wired for Success: The Leadership Journeys That Shaped Today's Top Technology Executives" will inspire and empower you. This book is a testament to the power of shared knowledge and the collective drive for excellence that binds these remarkable leaders.

Join us on this enlightening journey and discover the key learnings that have propelled these IT executives to the forefront of their field. Through their stories, may you find the inspiration and guidance to navigate your own path to success in the dynamic world of information technology.

When Jewels are in the Rough

The Art of Seeing Potential Others Miss

Dr. Denise Cornish

Mary, an administrative assistant in another department, was someone many of my team members routinely complained about working with. "She's so difficult," "She asks too many questions," "She's always asking for more information than she needs," "Who gives her this type of power?" were complaints I heard over and over. At that time, I hadn't worked with Mary that much. I was a new IT manager, though an employee of the organization I had worked for, for about four years. My team supported the other department from an enterprise application standpoint, though at the time, Mary and I never really interacted. But now as a new manager, I needed to work with Mary to accomplish certain organizational objectives. Based on what I had heard, I was dreading interacting with Mary.

As I approached Mary at the counter, letting her know what my intentions were and assuming that I, of course, knew all the answers, she immediately began asking me question after question—Oh man, my team was right, and I found myself getting more and more annoyed with Mary. But, as I began to answer her questions, I noticed that Mary had a gift of not only drawing out essential information but prescribing the appropriate pathways to move forward. Imagine that—an administrative assistant with no formal postsecondary training having a gift that takes many people formal education and years to master.

I noted Mary's unique ability and thought to myself, if I ever had the chance to hire Mary and bring her over to my department, I would find a place for her.

Over the course of the next few months, I found myself reaching out to Mary and seeking her input on process and software changes. It turns out, Mary knew the systems her department used inside and out and often had brilliant ideas that went unacted on. There is more to this story about Mary, whom I eventually courted over to my team and brought in as a key resource, but I had a light-bulb moment with this situation. First, Mary was a diamond that went unnoticed by her previous team. Second, that is when I realized that jewels can be found at all levels of an organization, and it is often those on the frontlines that ensure success in your organization if you give them a chance and help to develop their talents.

In this chapter, I'm excited to delve into the idea of finding the jewels in your team—whether diamonds, rubies, or other gems, they exist. Being intentional about helping people grow professionally was a step I accidentally took as a new leader, and it transformed my perspective. Join me as I share my journey through the art of discovery, nurturing and polishing jewels, and celebrating and retaining talent.

As for me and my beginning journey, working with Mary awakened something in me, the passion to dig into internal talent and find that untapped potential. Mary went on to do amazing things, contributing in ways even she did not realize she was capable of, and I found myself cheering her on and eventually mentoring her to later take on bigger and better job opportunities outside of the organization. I know what you may be thinking, why invest in someone so much that they end up leaving for bigger things? To that I say, investing in people and helping them reach their fullest potential is never a loss, it's a privilege. When we lift others up, we contribute to a ripple effect of growth and success that extends far beyond our organization. It's about creating a legacy of empowerment, not just retention.

The Art of Discovery—Recognizing Potential

Natalie Salaiz, my new administrative assistant, began her role with energy and enthusiasm, ready to support both me and the department. No task was beneath her, and she often came up with creative solutions to routine operational challenges. I took note. Though she mostly stayed quiet during meetings while taking minutes, it became clear to me that Natalie possessed sharp logic and strong critical thinking skills—she had something to contribute. I began inviting her to share her thoughts during meetings, which did three things: First, others noticed that I "dared" to seek input from an administrative assistant. Second, her insights helped advance our discussions, and I could see her confidence grow each time she spoke. And third—of course—the critics emerged, questioning why I was involving her at all. But their resistance only confirmed for me that Natalie was someone worth investing in. I thought back to Mary, who turned out to be a jewel for the organization and for herself. It was time to find out what else Natalie could do—and where she wanted to go.

As time went on, I gave Natalie more projects and greater decision-making authority to help manage the day-to-day operations of my office—and she was phenomenal. Any leader would have been grateful for that kind of support and reluctant to let it go. But her potential was impossible to ignore. Natalie had a gift: she communicated with confidence, absorbed new knowledge quickly, and used feedback to grow stronger.

One day, I approached her and said, "I can see you running this department someday. In fact, I can see you running the entire IT enterprise. If that's something you're interested in, and you stick with me, I promise that as long as I'm here, I'll support you and mentor you."

At the time, Natalie didn't have a degree, nor did she aspire to a leadership role in IT. But that conversation sparked something. She enrolled in school, earned her bachelor's degree, then her master's—and she didn't stop there. Everything she touched reflected excellence. And the best part? I wasn't the only one who saw it.

As I moved on from my role, Natalie stepped into it—and today, she leads the entire Information Technology unit. I couldn't be more excited and proud.

The art of discovery is about seeing beyond the surface—recognizing potential where others see routine and nurturing it into something extraordinary. With both Natalie and Mary, brilliance was there, waiting to be uncovered. Once I experienced the beauty and reward of identifying raw potential, I couldn't help myself—my mind and heart were constantly scanning for hidden jewels.

From my perspective, the art of discovery comes down to three things:

- **Active listening and observation:** As leaders, we must develop the ability to truly hear our team members and observe their actions. Often, strengths, aspirations, and potential aren't

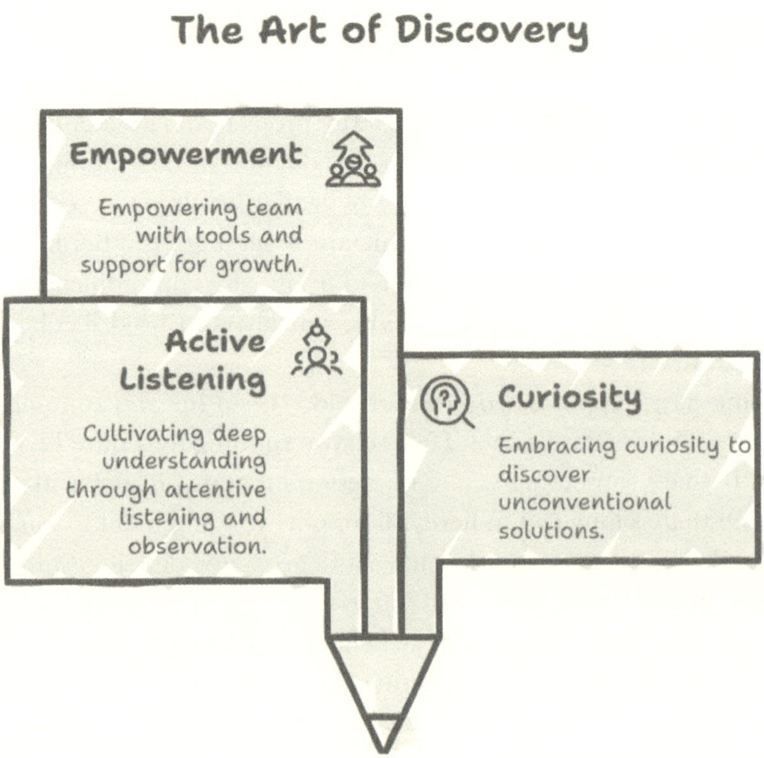

immediately visible—they emerge through presence and attention.

- **Curiosity and open-mindedness:** When team members show curiosity or offer unconventional approaches to problem-solving, recognize it for the gold it is. Embrace these thinkers, and you'll soon see their hidden talents and innovative ideas shine through.
- **Empowerment and support:** Give your team room to stretch. Provide them with the tools, mentorship, and encouragement to explore and develop their own brilliance. That's where transformation begins.

Nurturing and Polishing Jewels

In 2019, I was serving as Senior Director of Enterprise Applications & Databases, a subunit within the IT department. We were under new leadership, just two months in, when this new leader began including me in meetings and discussions well beyond my official responsibilities.

One day, as we walked back from a meeting, he turned to me and said, "I brought you into that room—and others—because I needed an innovative thinker."

Shortly after, he invested in me further by assigning me an executive coach to support my growth. For the first time in a long time, I felt truly seen. Someone believed in me enough to invest in my future—and I was elated.

Then 2020 arrived, and with it, the pandemic. That same leader asked me to head up our organization's COVID logistical support team. It was a daunting new responsibility, one that came with urgency and high stakes.

Before stepping into the role, he asked me who I thought could step in to lead the enterprise applications and database team in my absence. Without hesitation, I thought of Natalie. I moved her into the temporary role and focused all my energy on managing our pandemic response.

I knew—even then—that this was a test. And while I was nervous, I was also energized. I threw myself fully into the assignment, and in time, our COVID logistical support team was recognized for playing a critical role in keeping the organization running during one of its most challenging periods.

About six months into the role, I got an urgent message from my leader—he wanted to meet right away. My paranoid brain leapt to conclusions: I must've messed up so badly that I was about to be sent back to my old role—or worse. I remember thinking, "Well, the gig is up."

It wasn't. Quite the opposite.

I was officially promoted to Associate Vice President of Information Technology and Deputy Chief Operating Officer. With that, I permanently promoted Natalie to the director position I had vacated.

Only in hindsight did I realize what had happened: my leader had nurtured and polished me—and I, in turn, had done the same for Natalie.

Reflecting on that experience, I believe there are four key behaviors leaders must embrace to uncover and elevate hidden talent:

- **Recognize and elevate potential:** When my leader saw something in me beyond my current title, he brought me into strategic meetings. That trust validated my abilities and fueled my growth.
- **Create opportunities for stretch and impact:** Leading the COVID logistical support team was a career-defining moment. It pushed me far beyond my comfort zone—and into a space where I could make a real difference.
- **Invest in development:** Providing me with an executive coach strengthened my leadership skills and prepared me for broader responsibilities, including my current role as Senior Vice President and Chief Operating Officer.

- **Mentor and empower consistently:** My leader became my mentor—and his belief in me helped me thrive. I've done the same for Natalie, and she continues to exceed every expectation I had.

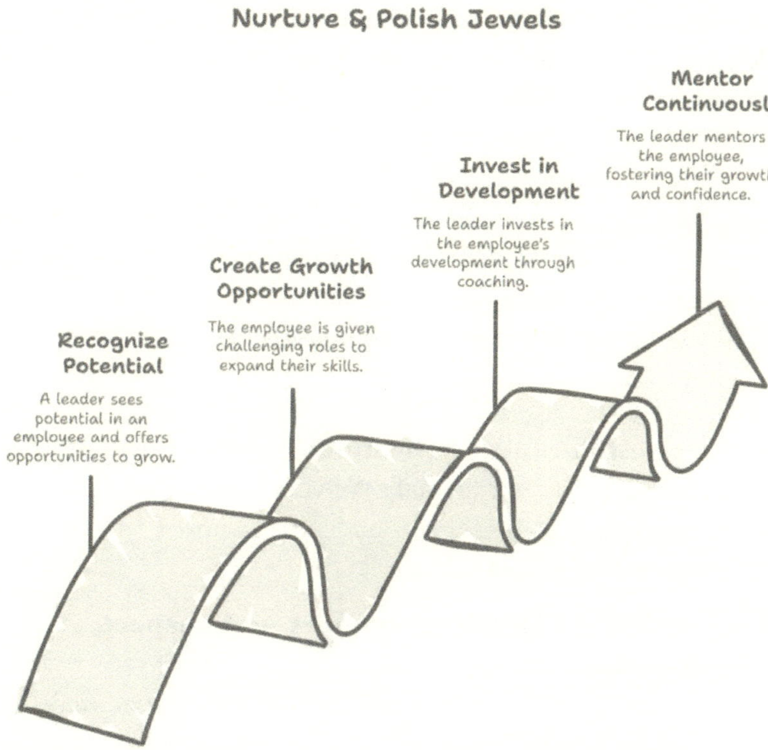

Celebrating, Retaining, and Letting Go

I've learned some hard lessons about what happens when you don't continue to celebrate your jewels—or do what's necessary to retain them. One of my biggest regrets is allowing my calendar to become so overloaded that I stopped making time to connect with the very people I had discovered and nurtured. I mistakenly believed that once they were in their roles, they no longer needed the same level of engagement from me. I began prioritizing other demands, assuming they could manage on their own.

But I've since realized I'm not alone in this misstep. Many seasoned leaders fall into the same trap—until they discover that some of their top talent is no longer as fulfilled, or worse, has begun exploring opportunities elsewhere.

I've come to liken this process to what can happen in romantic relationships after the courtship and honeymoon phase—when we get comfortable and stop doing the very things that helped the relationship flourish in the first place. The same can happen in leadership. We get busy. We assume our people are fine. But as leaders, it should come as no surprise: we must continue to celebrate those who bring everything together. We must uplift our teams, challenge them in meaningful ways, and be at peace when they move on.

Now, in this stage of my leadership journey and my role as a senior executive, experience has taught me four lasting lessons about celebrating, retaining, and releasing top talent:

- **Recognition and celebration:** Acknowledging individual and team wins is essential. We've all seen how recognition boosts morale and builds confidence. I know I wouldn't have grown the way I did without it.
- **Creating a culture of support and respect:** A strong team culture—where people feel they belong, are respected for their expertise, and know their contributions matter—is priceless. When a team feels connected, extraordinary things happen.
- **Being okay with letting go:** While I work hard to retain talent, I also take pride in watching team members grow into new roles beyond our organization. It's always a bittersweet moment, but one filled with pride. I celebrate their next chapter, knowing I played a part in their journey—and that my leadership ripple continues beyond our walls.
- **Taking satisfaction in the discovery:** Every time I see someone thrive after working alongside me, I'm reminded

why I lead the way I do. It's about finding the jewels, helping polish them, and then letting them shine wherever their path may lead.

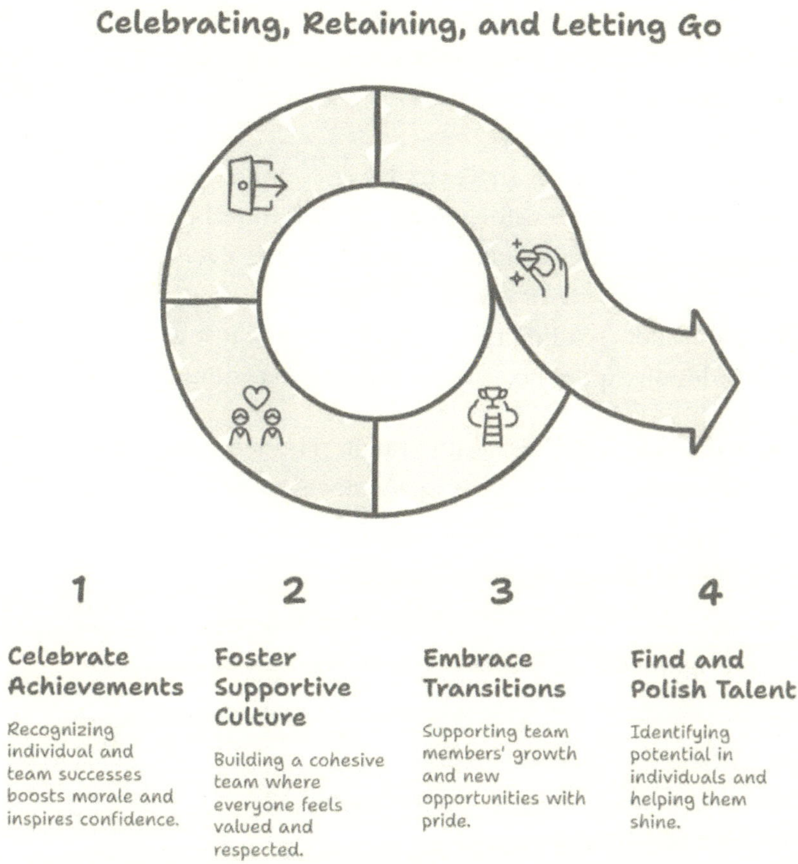

Conclusion and Call to Action

As I reflect on my leadership journey, I have come to realize that discovering the "jewels" within my team has been one of the most fulfilling parts of my career. It's not just about achieving success together in the moment, it's about shaping futures. Watching team members step into their brilliance, whether they continue within my team or move on to new opportunities, is a powerful reminder of the lasting impact leadership can have.

To me, true leadership is about recognizing potential, nurturing growth, and celebrating wins—both big and small. It's about taking quiet pride in knowing you have played a role in someone else's story. And when the time comes to let them go, it is about feeling joy—not loss—because you know they carry a part of your mentorship with them.

That's the legacy I strive to leave behind: one of discovery, empowerment, and transformation. And let me be clear—I'm still learning, still making mistakes, and still loving every minute of the journey.

To the leaders reading this—whether you're just getting started or have decades of experience—here's my call to action:

- Observe and listen with intent. Hidden jewels often reveal themselves in subtle, unexpected ways.
- Align opportunities with individual strengths. Give your team members roles that let them shine.
- Invest in their growth. Offer mentorship, training, and stretch assignments that challenge and inspire.
- Celebrate every success. Foster a culture of gratitude, acknowledgment, and encouragement.
- Let them go when the time comes. And take pride in the part you played in their journey.
- And most of all, remember: we are not the heroes of the story—our team members are.

Now, go out there and find the jewels in your team!

Call to Action

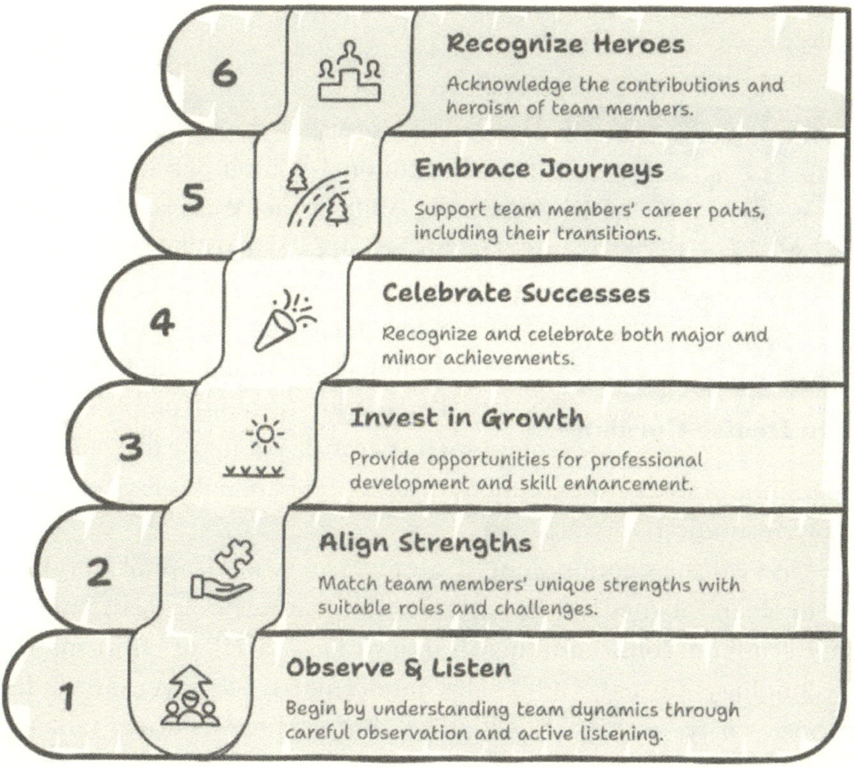

ABOUT THE AUTHOR

Dr. Denise Cornish

Dr. Denise Cornish is the Senior Vice President, Institutional Shared Services & Chief Operating Officer at Western University of Health Sciences, where she leads strategic operations across ten cross-functional departments, including Information Technology, Capital Planning, and Campus Safety. Known for turning complexity into clarity, Dr. Cornish is often called upon to align innovation with execution, creating operational ecosystems that move institutions forward.

She led the development of a university-wide Capital Improvement Plan aligned with accreditation, strategic growth, and a multi-million-dollar funding framework. As VP of Information Technology turned COO, she modernized IT governance, led cybersecurity readiness initiatives including executive tabletop exercises, and introduced AI governance to ensure safe and ethical innovation. Her leadership has unified diverse departments under a single strategic vision and established master planning efforts across two campuses.

Dr. Cornish is driven by the belief that operational excellence and human-centered leadership can—and should—coexist. She's passionate about breaking silos, building cohesion, and designing systems that serve both mission and momentum. Her edge? Turning operational chaos into coordinated action—without losing the human touch.

She's an active voice in national and international leadership circles, speaking at global technology and campus safety conferences and serving on advisory boards focused on innovation and digital transformation.

Dr. Cornish is building a future where operations are inclusive, tech-enabled, and always people-first. Her mantra? "We are not the heroes of this story—our teams are."

Outside of work, she recharges through travel and cherishes time spent with family and lifelong friends.

When I Look Back: Lessons from the Climb

Dan Lasher

The IT industry evolves at breakneck speed. To stay relevant and flourish, you must adapt, innovate, and position yourself as indispensable. Whether you're just launching your career or aiming to accelerate it, this chapter offers strategies to help you stand out, grow faster, and become a top performer.

Over my 37-year journey from entry-level IT to serving as CIO and CISO at a global high-tech firm, I've earned 18 promotions. That path wasn't luck. It was the result of grit, intentional career planning, and lessons learned from incredible mentors. I'll share what worked, what didn't, and how you can chart a trajectory of your own.

Career development roadmap

The IT field offers a wide range of technical and leadership roles where ambitious professionals can grow and thrive. My journey began over 30 years ago with a clear aspiration: to become a Chief Technology Officer, someone who leads with innovation, uses technology to solve complex problems, and drives organizational growth.

To reach that goal, I developed a career roadmap, a strategic plan to build the skills and experiences required for the role I envisioned. If you're aiming for a similar path, creating a roadmap of your own can be a powerful step forward. Here are the core components.

1. **Research the Role**: Study professionals who currently hold your target position. Learn from their paths, challenges, and achievements.
2. **Build Your Roadmap**: Assess your current skills, experience, and capabilities. Then identify the gaps—those become your to-do list.
3. **Work the Plan with Purpose**: Be intentional. Choose roles, projects, and challenges that directly align with your long-term goals.
4. **Know Your Core Strengths**: Lean into what you do best. Understanding and leveraging your natural strengths is a key advantage.
5. **Clarify Your Interests**: Think about the work that energizes you. These interests can help shape a career that is both successful and fulfilling.
6. **Track Industry Trends**: Stay informed about the needs and direction of your industry. Align your growth with where your field is headed.
7. **Identify Growth Areas**: Pinpoint areas for improvement or new skills you will need to reach your destination—and plan to close those gaps.

Once your career roadmap is in place, the next step is execution. Check in regularly, weekly if you can, and hold yourself accountable to your goals. With your plan as a guide, stay alert for opportunities that align with your trajectory.

Tip 1 – Be bold

Take risks. Big ones. Bold moves often create the biggest leaps forward.

At one point in my career, I was offered the chance to lead a failing web development project, one that had already consumed millions of dollars with little to show for it. The platform was flawed, and the entire initiative was about to be shelved, taking $20 million in sunk costs with it.

I saw potential. So I walked into the CIO's office and asked him to take off the handcuffs. I promised to deliver the functionality within three months for just $200,000. Then, quite literally, I slid my badge across the table and told him, "If I fail, you can keep it."

His response? "All right, hotshot. You've got three months."

We delivered the project on time, under budget, and it earned our team widespread recognition from customers and vendors. That bold move, and another like it, led to two major promotions.

Tip 2 – Be at the right place at the right time

Look for projects that can propel your career forward. Be brave, and do not hesitate when they appear. Sometimes, a once-in-a-lifetime opportunity shows up unannounced, and you must be ready to move.

Many of my own career leaps came from saying *yes* in critical, high-risk moments, often without a clear path to success.

One example: a major system outage occurred in France during the holidays. Most of the local IT staff were unreachable, and my CIO was preparing to fly out on Christmas Eve to handle it personally. I stepped in. "My bags are packed. I'll go," I said. It was not my area of responsibility, but I knew it was a moment that could define my career.

Another time, I saw a merger and acquisition project going off course. Despite having no experience with technical due diligence or data center consolidation, I volunteered to take over. The executive visibility was intense, and the risks were high—but I knew this was exactly the kind of experience that would move me closer to a C-level role.

These moments did not come with guarantees. But seizing them paid off.

Tip 3 – Do the tough things

Some of the greatest career accelerators come from tackling the challenges others avoid. When you lean into difficult, high-stakes situations, you build a reputation for being fearless, and results-driven.

In summary, whether you're an individual contributor or in a leadership role, the formula is the same: be bold, seize opportunities, and take on the tough assignments. These are the moments that get noticed and remembered.

Make yourself sought after and indispensable

In IT, job security does not come from playing it safe. It comes from being the person your organization can't afford to lose. Develop specialized skills, stay ahead of trends, and build a reputation for delivering results.

Equally important? Your attitude. One mindset that has served me well: *We don't have problems—we have opportunities.* Every outage, every challenge, every fire drill is a chance to grow, lead, and win. When you consistently show up with this kind of mindset, people notice, and you become the person they call first when it really matters.

Seek rapid growth

Stagnation is the enemy of progress. High-performing IT professionals don't wait for promotions to fall into their laps, they actively seek out growth. They pursue mentors, expand their skill sets, and volunteer for tough assignments that stretch their capabilities.

Early in my career, I made it a habit to chase the most complex, high-risk, and business-critical projects. I knew staying in my comfort zone wouldn't get me far. I took on initiatives others avoided, stepped into failed projects to turn them around, and made my case to CIOs to lead efforts I knew would challenge me.

These moves weren't random; they were all part of a broader strategy. I used my career development plan as a roadmap to identify and close gaps in my technical, business, and leadership skills. Every project was a stepping stone toward the next level.

Your career will only grow as fast as your ability to contribute to your team's success and to the company's bottom line. Advancement isn't just about personal accomplishments; it's about aligning your work with business outcomes. Here are a few tips to keep your contributions relevant and recognized.

Tip 1 – Relevance

Always connect IT deliverables to real business needs. If you're delivering wins that no one asked for—or doesn't understand—you risk wasting effort and losing credibility. Solve problems that matter.

Tip 2 – Partner

Build relationships with business stakeholders, customers, and even competitors. Use data and competitive insights to guide your priorities and build trust. When stakeholders see your impact, they become your advocates.

Tip 3 – Recognition

Great leaders succeed by helping others thrive. Celebrate team wins loudly and often. And don't shy away from spotlighting failures. They're often the turning points that lead to deeper learning and future success.

Stand out and stay ahead

In a field full of capable professionals, standing out isn't optional. It's essential. Whether you specialize in a niche technology, lead with emotional intelligence, or bridge gaps across teams, your distinct value is what sets you apart.

Your goal? Become the person others turn to by differentiating yourself.

1. Identify career propellants
2. Take risks
3. Seek the complex assignments
4. Be the ultimate team player
5. Create momentum with monthly noteworthy wins
6. Execute
7. Have everyone think of you when something tough needs to be solved.

Take on high-risk projects – Volunteer for the tough assignments, such as rolling out a new system under tight deadlines or leading a turn-around project. These stretch moments accelerate growth and show you are ready to lead.

Embrace risk – Those "badge on the table" moments, where you put your name and reputation behind a bold move, signal courage and conviction. Even if the outcome isn't perfect, the act earns respect and visibility.

Be indispensable – Consistently deliver results, build strong relationships, and keep sharpening your skills. Critical projects and career opportunities start coming to you when you're known for your expertise and reliability.

Be a great teammate – Work hard, stay humble, and give credit where it's due. People notice. A strong work ethic paired with generosity of spirit goes a long way in building trust and influence.

Create wins – Make a habit of generating one meaningful "win" every month, something that helps your leader shine and moves your organization forward. That kind of steady momentum builds your brand as a high-impact performer.

Know your environment

Not all IT organizations are created equal. Industry, leadership, and company culture all shape how IT is perceived, and how much room you have to grow.

One key to career growth is understanding where your organization falls on the IT maturity curve. For example, if your team is seen only as a support function, focused purely on uptime and performance, your path to influence may be narrow.

If, on the other hand, IT is viewed as a strategic partner, there's likely more opportunity to drive change, lead initiatives, and step into a leadership role. Knowing the landscape helps you shape your strategy and set realistic, ambitious goals for where (and how) to grow.

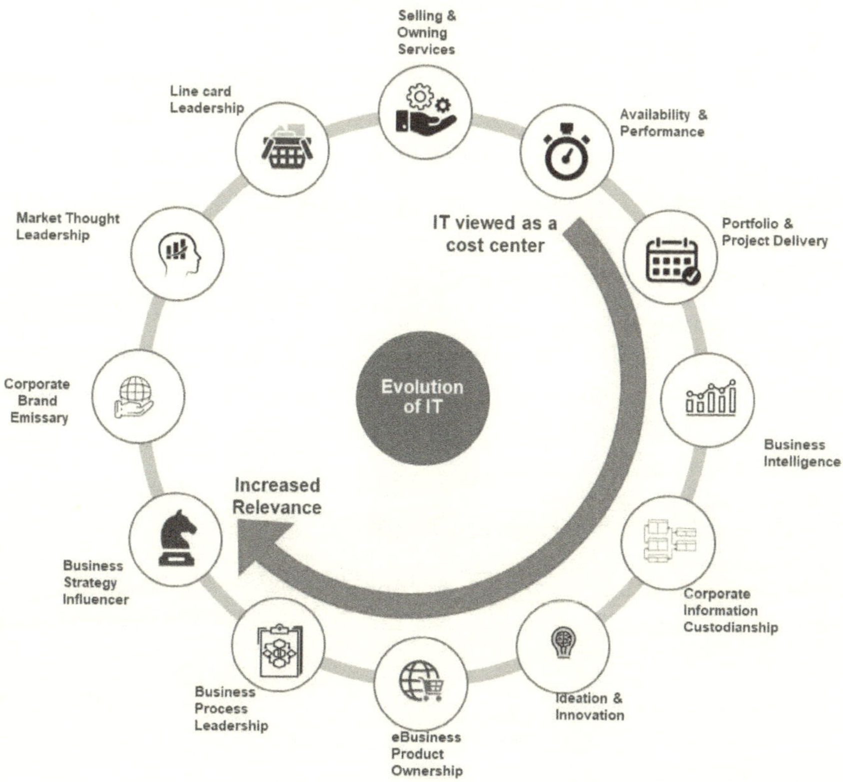

IT maturity evolves in stages, each reflecting the organization's perception of IT and its strategic role. At the lowest level, IT is seen as a cost center—focused on keeping the lights on. Efforts are reactive, centered around system availability and performance, with little room (or expectation) for innovation or strategic contribution.

As IT matures, the focus shifts from uptime to outcomes. The next phase emphasizes project and portfolio delivery—getting initiatives done on time and on budget through solid project management.

From there, IT evolves into a driver of digital products and eBusiness. Teams collaborate across functions to develop customer-facing solutions that deliver measurable business value.

At the highest level, IT steps into a strategic spotlight, shaping market trends, enhancing the corporate brand, and acting as a thought leader. Technology leaders at this stage don't just serve the business—they help define where it's going.

An IT organization's maturity level has a direct impact on your ability to grow. In high-functioning environments, strong performers can thrive and accelerate quickly. But in organizations where IT is still seen purely as a cost center, even the most capable leaders may find their growth stalled.

One of the most valuable pieces of advice I give aspiring leaders is this: choose your environment wisely. The right company culture and IT maturity can make all the difference. And if your growth is consistently blocked by structural limitations and not performance, it may be time to move on.

Building high performance teams

There is no shortage of books on building high-performance teams, but few offer a practical, day-to-day guide for putting those principles into action.

Looking back on my 37-year career, I have found that the most effective teams are built on balance. High performance does not require every individual to excel in every area, it requires a team where each member brings complementary strengths. The right mix of depth, breadth, experience, and skill across the group is what creates real momentum.

- Problem Solving
- Creating a collaborative environment
- Customer affinity and delight
- Authentic
- Analytical
- Ideation
- Communication skills
- Delegation and control
- Continuous learner
- Self-aware
- Partnership and Relationship building
- Delivers results
- Technical background
- Strategic thinking
- Leadership style
- Power of Persuasion
- Tell the story, sell an investment/idea
- Business acumen
- Decision speed
- Decision quality

It's the leader's responsibility to ensure the team includes individuals who collectively bring expertise and proficiency across all key dimensions.

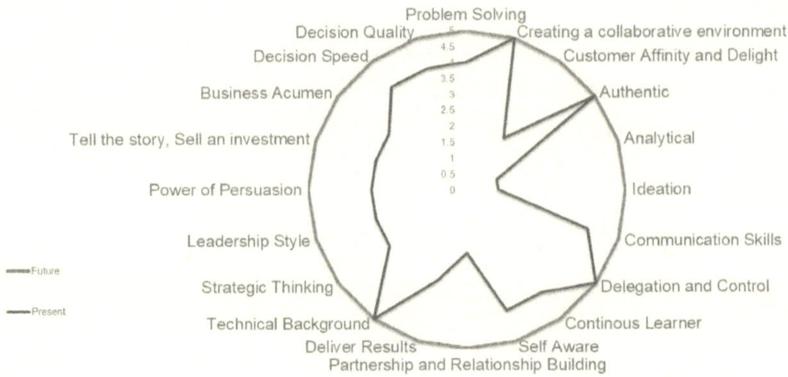

The diagram above illustrates the gap between a team's current capabilities (in black) and its future potential (in red) across a range of essential leadership and performance dimensions. It's a snapshot of what a balanced, high-performing team might strive to become.

In this example, the team is rich in technical skill but lacks strength in key areas such as analytical thinking, ideation, communication, storytelling, and relationship-building. Even the most technically brilliant team will fall short if it can't develop and articulate solutions, build cross-functional partnerships, or gain buy-in from decision-makers.

High-performing teams aren't just smart, they're strategically built. That means hiring, coaching, and mentoring with intent to round out your collective capabilities. Leaders must look beyond individual excellence and ask: Does my team collectively cover the full range of skills needed to move the organization forward?

In this case, rather than hiring yet another technical expert, the savvy leader would focus on filling the gaps, elevating such areas as business acumen, influence, and collaboration. Leaders who shape teams this way position themselves and their organizations for outsized impact.

If you aspire to lead at a high level, build a team where every dimension of performance has a standout contributor. Where gaps exist, close them through thoughtful development or strategic hiring. It's not about perfection, it's about balance, growth, and alignment with the mission ahead.

Be a goal driven leader

To fuel your personal growth as a leader, you must consistently set, monitor, and track progress against both individual and organizational goals. Goal setting should be second nature, an instinctive part of how you drive results, lead change, and move toward your vision.

Be sure to include a mix of bold "moonshot" goals, those that stretch your limits, and more achievable objectives with a clear path to execution. This balance keeps you both challenged and grounded, supporting momentum over time.

Define your goals with clarity: what success looks like, how it will be measured, and when it should be delivered. The more precise your roadmap, the more intentional your progress will be.

For example, a well-defined goal might look like this:

> ***Goal name*** strives to ***describe goal*** which will result in ***intended results*** which will be measured by ***measurement criteria*** within ***defined timeframe***.

That translates into this:

Increase customer satisfaction by 20% within the next six months by implementing a new customer feedback system and training staff on best practices for customer service. This will be measured by conducting monthly customer satisfaction surveys and tracking the percentage increase in positive feedback.

By setting clear, meaningful goals, you not only accelerate your own career growth, you also signal your leadership potential and commitment to driving positive outcomes across your organization.

To make goal setting truly effective, consider the following:

Be selective and strategic. Goals should challenge you, but remain attainable. One or two ambitious "moonshot" targets are fine, but most of your goals should be designed to move your organization forward steadily. Balance bold vision with realistic execution.

Align actions with purpose. Goals are just the start. Your action plans and methods bring them to life. Plan your weeks intentionally. Prioritize meetings, tasks, and decisions that support your objectives.

Review regularly. Set aside time each week to assess your progress. Reflect on wins, roadblocks, and challenges. Use those insights to adjust your next steps and maintain forward momentum.

In my own experience, cascading clear goals throughout the organization, and helping people connect their daily work to those goals, creates alignment, focus, and results. Every Friday, I review my own objectives and shape the following week's plan to ensure I'm moving closer to the outcomes I want to achieve. That discipline has made a measurable difference in both my leadership effectiveness and career progression.

Daily retrospective

One of the most valuable habits you can adopt is a daily retrospective. At the end of each day, take a moment to reflect by asking yourself: *If I could relive today, what would I do differently?* Or consider it through the lens of someone you admire: *If [insert name] were in my position today, what would they have done?*

This simple but powerful practice has been part of my routine for 37 years. It's helped me examine missteps, missed opportunities, and leadership blind spots—and, just as importantly, to recognize what went well. Over time, this habit fosters greater emotional intelligence, self-awareness, and wisdom.

When a key insight emerges, I jot it down in a journal. These reflections become fuel for personal growth, goal setting, and leadership evolution.

Be a leader that people admire

I've had the honor of receiving several industry awards, recognitions made possible by the incredible peers and teams I've worked alongside. You can find more details on my LinkedIn profile, but I share that not to boast, rather to highlight this: leadership is about delivering results *and* showing up for your team—supporting, growing, and championing the people around you.

While entire libraries are dedicated to leadership theory, the best leaders I've known consistently follow a few core principles:

- Build diverse teams with varied perspectives.
- Celebrate wins publicly and treat failures as opportunities to learn.
- Make performance reviews regular, honest, and constructive.
- Listen deeply—value every voice on the team.
- Identify high-potential talent early and invest in their development.
- Keep a pulse on leadership readiness and pipeline gaps.
- Establish succession plans for all key roles.
- Rotate top performers through new challenges to build depth.
- Encourage mentorship and active involvement in developing successors.
- Offer training in servant leadership, emotional intelligence, and communication.
- Create hands-on opportunities for emerging leaders to grow.
- Know your team—amplify their strengths and support their development areas.

- Clear obstacles so your team can move fast and thrive.
- Communicate clearly, consistently, and with purpose.
- Dream boldly, share your vision, and bring people along.
- Shine the spotlight on your team's successes—and own the failures when they happen.

Lead with humility, humanity, and high standards—and people will not only follow you, but they'll also grow because of you.

Process mastery

As a leader, you're accountable for results, and achieving those results depends on getting the right balance of people, processes, and technology. While technology gets much of the spotlight, true leadership requires a deep understanding of the business processes that drive your company, your department, and the cross-functional work in between.

No matter what the industry, mastering these processes gives you credibility. It helps you speak the language of business stakeholders, which opens doors to collaboration, influence, and strategic impact.

But this goes beyond simply knowing the steps in a workflow. It's about understanding how processes connect, where they create friction, and how they contribute to, or hinder, strategic goals. With this insight, you can streamline operations, spot improvement opportunities, and make decisions that align with the bigger picture.

Equally important, process fluency strengthens your partnerships across the organization. When you understand how work flows between teams, you foster better communication, stronger collaboration, and shared success.

Bottom line: leading through process mastery helps you deliver value, build trust, and position yourself as not just an IT leader, but a trusted business strategist.

Example processes:

- Procure to Pay
- Order to Cash
- Record to Report
- Hire to Retain
- Incident to Resolution
- Develop to Deploy
- Plan to Procure
- Marketing to Sales

Processes vary by industry, but regardless of the sector, I've made it a priority to understand them inside and out, especially how they connect to the broader supply chain, from customers to vendors. This depth of understanding has made me far more effective as a leader.

Over the years, I've job-shadowed people in logistics, sales, credit, marketing, purchasing, finance, HR, and more. Learning directly from those on the front lines gave me a clearer view of how the entire organization works and, importantly, allowed me to speak the language of each business function.

If you're serious about accelerating your career, I encourage you to do the same. Immersing yourself in how the business operates will set you apart, make you more valuable to your organization, and open doors to leadership opportunities.

The power of networking

Throughout my career, I've placed a high value on building a strong professional network—within my own organization, across industries, and with peers and thought leaders. Surrounding yourself with people who are smarter, more experienced, or offer different perspectives is one of the fastest ways to grow.

Every interaction is an opportunity to learn. Whether it's about leadership, process improvement, emerging technologies, financial or business strategy, or industry trends, stay curious. Continuous learning through meaningful relationships is a powerful tool for professional development and long-term success.

Beware of career advancement landmines

As you push toward your goals, be mindful of the behaviors that can quietly undermine your progress. Here are some of the most common pitfalls I've observed that can derail a promising career:

- **Don't multitask in meetings** – Be fully present. Close the laptop, put away distractions, and engage in active listening. People notice who's really in the room.
- **Honor your commitments** – Treat every promise like a contract. Deliver what you said, when you said you would. Under promise and overdeliver whenever possible.
- **Avoid "anecdotal terrorism"** – Use data responsibly. Ensure your facts are accurate and challenge others to do the same. "Shards" of facts and politically spun data damage trust and credibility.
- **Be a decent human** – Talent isn't enough. Leaders who are kind, respectful, and self-aware tend to build loyal, high-performing teams. Consider using 360-degree feedback to check how others truly experience you.
- **Be friendly, not overly familiar** – Today's peer might be your direct report tomorrow. Share wisely. Don't disclose anything you wouldn't share with your CEO. Use external networks for vulnerable or strategic conversations and consider the Chatham House Rule when needed.
- **Understand the levers of control** – IT leaders must manage time, budget, scope, quality, risk, and resources. Business

partners can drive one of these, not all. Clear communication about trade-offs is essential to success.

- **Know your "First Team"** – As Patrick Lencioni emphasizes in *The Five Dysfunctions of a Team*, your first loyalty should be to the team you're part of, not the one you lead. As your role evolves, so will your First Team. Be intentional about aligning with them.
- **Show up polished and professional** – Project the role you aspire to. How you speak, dress, behave, and manage emotions should reflect the next level you're aiming for. You're building credibility every day, so make it count.

In Summary

Over the course of my 37-year career in IT, spanning 18 promotions and numerous industry accolades, I've learned that sustained growth and success are never accidental. They're the result of deliberate planning, bold decisions, constant learning, and an unshakable commitment to excellence.

My hope is that the insights and experiences shared here will help illuminate your own path forward.

To recap, here are the key principles that shaped my journey:

- Create and follow a career development roadmap
- Make yourself indispensable
- Pursue rapid growth through stretch opportunities
- Stand out by differentiating your skills and value
- Understand how your organization's structure impacts your growth
- Build and lead high-performance teams
- Be a goal-driven leader with measurable outcomes
- Embrace a daily retrospective practice

- Be the kind of leader others admire and want to follow
- Master the processes that power your business
- Cultivate a strong, diverse professional network
- Steer clear of career-limiting pitfalls

Apply these lessons with intention, and you'll not only grow your career, you'll elevate those around you and leave a legacy of impact.

ABOUT THE AUTHOR

Dan Lasher

Dan Lasher has served in numerous roles in the IT industry for 37 years. He currently is the CIO and CISO at D&H Distribution, a leading technology distributor of IT and electronics offering end-to-end solutions for today's reseller and retailer and the clients they serve across the SMB and Consumer markets. Prior to D&H, Mr. Lasher was CISO and in key roles that included Chief Architect and Innovation Leader at TD SYNNEX, a $64B global distributor.

Dan has led numerous successful global projects for digital innovation, ERP migrations, technology projects and has two decades of intense Cyber Security experience combatting nation state threat actors and global hacktivists while protecting a critical supply chain.

Known for building high performance teams, Dan combines visionary strategy with extraordinary execution. His teams describe him as a servant leader who coaches and mentors his teams to win, grow and flourish. His peers and colleagues have nominated him for numerous awards, leading to winning Security Professional of the Year and Technology Executive of the Year, Tampa Bay.

Dan has served on numerous boards including FBI Infragard, University of South Florida Advisory Board and Tampa Bay Technology Forum.

Outside of work, you will find him giving back to the community through coaching and mentoring aspiring talent in the field of IT, providing instruction for inner city single mothers on Cyber Security curriculum, as well as spending time with his grandchildren.

When Vulnerability Builds Strength

Kelly Solomon

Being vulnerable is difficult and uncomfortable for me, but I'm going to do it anyway. I want to share one of the most painful yet valuable lessons I have ever learned.

Throughout our lives, we encounter people through circumstance. As children and young adults, we're surrounded by classmates. In the working world, we're surrounded by colleagues. Someone once told me she knew a coworker had become a true friend when they started spending time together outside of work. That idea has always stuck with me.

One of those meaningful relationships in my life was with a lawyer-turned-legal-librarian named Holliday Gordon. Holliday was smart, wickedly funny, and a joy to work with. We collaborated on countless projects supporting attorneys at a boutique law firm in Atlanta. Over time, a genuine friendship formed.

Holliday and I bonded over lunches that soon turned into after-work drinks, online gaming sessions, and weekend outings to museums. Somewhere along the way, she was diagnosed with cancer. It wasn't her first battle. She had fought it before, but this time was different. This was a fight she wouldn't win. As often happens in these situations, some friends began to fade into the background. People sometimes don't know how to be present when someone they care about is struggling.

On Friday nights, I'd pick up burritos and head over to Holliday's house, where we'd hang out and watch *Say Yes to the Dress*. During those visits, she opened up to me, sharing her thoughts, her fears, and what she believed was ahead as she faced death. These were conversations she couldn't have with just anyone. Mortality isn't an easy topic, and not everyone is comfortable confronting it. But I didn't try to fix it. I simply listened.

At the same time, I was navigating a painful divorce from an abusive marriage. Compared to cancer, my struggles felt trivial, almost silly. But Holliday wanted to hear about them. There's something deeply comforting about simple rituals: burritos and bad TV with a friend who truly listens. During one of those evenings, I shared details of my marriage I had never told anyone. I remember the moment vividly. Holliday's appetite had faded, and she barely touched the massive burrito in front of her. While Randy buzzed on the screen, gushing over a bride and giving her that signature "zhuzh," Holliday sat quietly, her expression suddenly serious.

"I used to envy you," she said.

I must have looked completely bewildered. Holiday explained that when she met me, she saw someone who was smart, confident, and seemed to have the perfect marriage and picture-perfect home life.

My heart shattered.

The idea that, in her too-short life, Holliday had envied something that wasn't real was devastating. Without meaning to, I had hurt my friend by maintaining a façade. That moment changed me. It forced me to see how much damage I was doing to myself and to others by always putting on a brave face, by always answering "I'm fine" when I wasn't.

In that moment, I made a quiet vow to show up more honestly with others. The truth is, everything isn't always fine. Pretending otherwise only builds walls. I learned that vulnerability doesn't weaken us; it humanizes us. And in that shared humanity, real connection begins.

Vulnerability. Merriam-Webster defines it as *capable of being wounded* and *open to attack or damage.* On the surface, it certainly sounds like a weakness. But in reality, vulnerability is one of the most transformative qualities a leader can possess. It builds trust, deepens relationships, and strengthens teams in ways that traditional management strategies often fall short.

The significance of vulnerability was further cemented for me in 2019, when my family experienced an unimaginable tragedy. A man broke into my parents' home, killed my brother and a friend of my niece, and then took his own life. The horror made international headlines, turning our private pain into a public spectacle.

I felt exposed. Everything was *not* fine, and would never be the same again. It felt like I was walking through life with an open, festering wound that everyone could see… and possibly judge.

That experience taught me the nuances of vulnerability. While sharing is essential for building a genuine connection, it's equally important to gauge whether others are ready (or able) to receive your truth. Just as Holliday wanted to talk about death and what she believed was coming, not everyone in her life was prepared for those conversations. And that's okay. Vulnerability requires both courage from the speaker and readiness from the listener.

Listening is a critical part of vulnerability. We have to create space for others to share their stories and unseen burdens. When we truly listen—without judgment or interruption—we show that we value their experiences and perspectives. We don't have to agree. We don't even have to respond. Sometimes, simply being present and engaged is enough to foster a real connection.

That connection, in turn, is powerful. When people feel understood and supported, they're more likely to go the extra mile. Teams that feel seen collaborate more effectively and dare to innovate with greater confidence.

As a leader, I've found that vulnerability requires balance. It means acknowledging mistakes, sharing struggles, and showing humanity without placing too much emotional weight on others. People are drawn to leaders who are real, who admit they don't have all the answers but are committed to finding them together. Vulnerability builds trust, and trust is the foundation of every strong team.

My mother once told me, "We all have a choice. We can either lay down and die, or we can just keep going." Her words have stayed with me, especially in moments when life felt unbearable. Over time, I've come to understand that "just keep going" doesn't mean pushing forward alone. It means asking for help when needed—and giving others the opportunity to step up and support you. Ben Franklin's advice echoes this: ask your rivals for favors.

"I need your help." These four words carry immense power. They tap into a basic human desire: to be needed, to feel useful, to play the hero. Even a rival, when asked for a favor, becomes invested in your success. Suddenly, competition becomes cooperation, and a connection forms. Asking for help is not a weakness; it's a strategic act that fuels relationships, fosters goodwill, and unlocks unexpected alliances. Know when to let others step in, not just for your benefit, but for theirs.

Leadership isn't about projecting perfection; it's about revealing humanity. Life's challenges, from personal tragedies to professional missteps, offer powerful opportunities to connect and inspire. It's hard to stay angry at someone who openly admits their mistakes and takes responsibility. Vulnerability invites others to do the same, creating a culture rooted in trust, mutual respect, and continuous learning. When we listen, share, and support one another, we build teams that are resilient and capable of overcoming any obstacle together.

Vulnerability isn't a weakness; it's a strength. It allows us to lead with authenticity, forge meaningful connections, and foster a culture where people feel seen, valued, and motivated. As leaders, our greatest impact doesn't come from titles or achievements, but from the relationships we build and the lives we influence. By embracing vulnerability, we can lead with both courage and compassion, and in doing so, we inspire others to do the same.

ABOUT THE AUTHOR

Kelly Solomon

Architect of Transformation: Building Teams, Driving Change, Delivering Results

Kelly Solomon is the Vice President of Enterprise Architecture at Vestis, bringing over 30 years of experience leading teams and driving transformation to deliver business success. Following Vestis' $2.7B divestiture from Aramark, Kelly built the company's Enterprise Architecture function from the ground up, aligning technology strategy with enterprise goals. She is known for influencing change, building high-performing teams, and leading with integrity and authenticity. Kelly holds an MBA and multiple industry certifications.

At Vestis, Kelly developed an ROI-driven intake framework that strategically allocates company time, talent, and resources. She directed cross-functional teams through the technological complexities of the divestiture and drove service innovation, including launching an industry-first customer notification platform that improved satisfaction and retention.

Kelly is results-driven, fueled by a passion for continuous improvement and helping others realize their potential. She believes transformation is a journey and is committed to building environments where integrity and trust are the foundations of growth and success.

Known for her practical leadership style, Kelly has been described as consummately kind yet devastatingly effective — able to break large-scale initiatives into sprints and deliver transformational results before others realize the full impact.

Her guiding belief? "Transformation is a journey. Keep going."

Kelly is also a passionate mentor for women in technology, an avid traveler and golfer, and enjoys life with her husband, Francis, and three cats.

When Lessons Were Learned as an IT Leader

Kamal Mohanty

"In my years of leadership, I've learned that tech problems are easy; people problems are the real code to crack. Firewalls won't block bad communication, AI can't replace emotional intelligence (yet), and no amount of automation can fix a culture resistant to change."

– Kamal Mohanty

25 Years, Countless Lessons, and Yes, a Few "What Was I Thinking?" Moments

If there's one thing I've learned in my 25-year rollercoaster ride through the corporate and IT world, it's that *leadership and management are two very different beasts*. Sure, keeping the servers running and the projects on schedule is important, but true leadership? That's about inspiring innovation, navigating chaos, and occasionally convincing an entire organization that yes, the change is a good idea.

This chapter isn't just a collection of tech war stories—it's a playbook for IT leadership, built on real-world wins, the occasional facepalm moment, and the kind of insights that only come from living through the digital revolution firsthand. Leading in IT isn't just about knowing your APIs from your KPIs—it's about strategy, emotional intelligence, adaptability, and knowing when to nod knowingly in a boardroom full of buzzwords.

Through real-world insights, practical strategies, and personal reflections, I aim to provide aspiring and current IT executives with guidance on how to lead effectively, inspire their teams, and make a lasting impact. Whether you are stepping into your first leadership role or are a seasoned executive looking for fresh perspectives, I hope these lessons will serve as a valuable resource in your leadership journey.

I invite you to explore these insights with an open mind, reflect on your own experiences, and apply these principles to enhance your effectiveness as an IT leader.

Lesson 1: Leadership is About People, Not Just Technology

One of the most profound lessons I have learned in IT leadership is realizing that *technology doesn't drive transformation—people do.* Sure, technical expertise is important, but the best strategy, the most cutting-edge tools, and the most well-architected systems mean nothing if the people implementing them aren't engaged, empowered, and aligned with the vision. Leadership isn't about knowing every line of code—it's about knowing how to inspire the people who write it.

Leaders don't just give orders—they listen, they mentor, and they celebrate wins, big and small. After all, a high-performing team isn't built on just skill sets, but on trust, communication, and shared purpose.

At the end of the day, servers crash, systems break, and projects get delayed—but strong leadership ensures that teams stay motivated, resilient, and ready to tackle whatever challenge comes next. Because in IT, as in life, the biggest competitive advantage is not just technology, it's the people behind it.

Key Takeaways:

1. **Listen Actively**: Works in every aspect of our lives. Understand the needs, concerns, and aspirations of your team members. Active listening builds trust and strengthens relationships.
2. **Recognize Contributions**: Celebrate individual and team achievements to foster morale and motivation.

3. **Cultivate Empathy**: I am a compassionate and practical person. I have always believed that a compassionate approach to leadership creates a positive and supportive work environment.

My experience, where I applied it and how I learned this valuable lesson

During a global cloud migration at one of the world's largest beverage companies, my team had the *refreshing* challenge of moving Freestyle beverage system data and analytics to Microsoft Azure and AWS—because, apparently, real-time insights pair well with every drink. Just when we thought we had it all figured out, legacy ERP systems and IoT-connected dispensers decided to throw a tantrum, causing unexpected delays. Instead of letting chaos fizz over, I tapped into active listening, recognition, and empathy like a secret ingredient. I hosted cross-functional listening sessions—part IT therapy, part strategy reboot—bringing engineers, supply chain managers, and marketing teams together to realign priorities before things went flat. To keep spirits high, I made a habit of publicly celebrating wins in leadership meetings and newsletters, because nothing fuels motivation like well-earned recognition. Knowing this was a global effort, I introduced flexible work shifts and extra resources to prevent burnout, creating a collaborative, solution-oriented culture. In the end, we not only poured the perfect blend of technology and teamwork, but we also cut operational costs by 30% and unlocked predictive analytics for customer insights and supply chain forecasting. Moral of the story? Even the best IT transformations need the right mix of strategy, engagement, and a people-first approach to avoid going flat.

Lesson 2: Align Technology with Business Goals

IT is not an isolated function but a core driver of business success. The most effective IT executives ensure that their strategies and initiatives are tightly aligned with organizational objectives.

Key Takeaways:

1. **Understand the Business**: Invest time in learning about the organization's goals, challenges, and industry dynamics.
2. **Bridge the Gap**: Translate technical capabilities into business value by demonstrating how technology solutions support revenue growth, cost savings, or customer satisfaction.
3. **Speak the Language of the Boardroom**: Avoid technical jargon when communicating with non-technical stakeholders and focus on outcomes that matter to them.

My experience, where I applied it and how I learned this valuable lesson:

During a global ERP modernization project, I quickly realized that *throwing new tech at old problems was like putting a fresh coat of paint on a sinking ship*—it looked good, but the real issues ran deeper. While IT teams were laser-focused on system upgrades, a few conversations with finance, operations, and sales leaders revealed the real culprits—manual workflows slower than a dial-up connection, revenue leaks big enough to drain a budget, and order fulfillment inefficiencies that made customers question reality. Instead of just geeking out over system specs, I rebranded IT's role—positioning the ERP as a revenue accelerator, not just a software upgrade. When it came time to pitch the executive board, I swapped out the technical jargon for language they actually cared about—ROI, cost savings, and operational efficiency. Suddenly, the ERP wasn't just an IT expense—it was a profitability playbook. The result? Executive buy-in, smoother adoption, and an IT transformation that didn't just check a box, but actually moved the business forward. Lesson learned: tech is never the hero—business impact is.

Lesson 3: Embrace Change and Adaptability

In the fast-paced world of technology, change isn't just inevitable—it's the only constant. Whether it's the rise of AI, the shift to cloud computing, or the latest cybersecurity threats, the IT landscape is in perpetual evolution. Effective IT leaders don't just react to change; they anticipate it, embrace it, and leverage it as a competitive advantage. Rather than seeing disruption as a roadblock, they view it as a chance to innovate, streamline operations, and create new value for the business.

Key Takeaways:

1. **Be a Change Advocate**: Lead by example and demonstrate a willingness to embrace new technologies, processes, and perspectives.
2. **Stay Flexible**: Be prepared to pivot strategies in response to evolving circumstances.
3. **Prepare Your Team**: Equip your team with the skills and mindset needed to navigate change successfully.

My experience, where I applied it and how I learned this valuable lesson:

In the early days of cloud adoption, I quickly realized that *pushing new tech without changing mindsets was like trying to sell a self-driving car to someone who still loves their horse and buggy*. Resistance was inevitable—teams clung to their legacy apps like treasured antiques. So, instead of just preaching the cloud gospel, I became the first convert—ditching outdated tools and showcasing cloud-based collaboration in action. Just when we thought we had momentum, compliance roadblocks popped up like unexpected plot twists, forcing us to pivot without derailing progress. Rather than let fear of change slow us down, I doubled down on upskilling—launching hands-on workshops, mentorship programs, and training sessions that transformed skeptics into cloud champions. Sure, some migrations ran a little behind schedule, but when the dust settled, adoption was through the roof. The biggest lesson? *Cloud transformation wasn't just about technology—it's about getting people to embrace the sky instead of clinging to the ground.*

Lesson 4: Build Strong Cross-Functional Relationships

In IT, success isn't just about having the best tech—it's about having the right people on board. No matter how groundbreaking an initiative is, if finance won't approve it, operations can't integrate it, or sales doesn't see the value, it's dead on arrival. Collaboration isn't a nice-to-have—it's the secret sauce that turns IT projects into business wins.

Building strong relationships across departments means speaking their language, not just tech jargon. When IT stops being a silo and becomes a strategic partner, initiatives move faster, adoption increases, and innovation thrives. Because at the end of the day, the best IT solutions don't just work—they work for everyone.

Key Takeaways:

1. **Foster Open Communication**: Create channels for regular dialogue and feedback with other departments.
2. **Understand Their Needs**: Take time to understand the priorities and challenges of other teams to provide tailored solutions.
3. **Break Down Silos**: Encourage collaboration by involving cross-functional teams in technology planning and implementation.

My experience, where I applied it and how I learned this valuable lesson:

During an enterprise-wide CRM implementation, I leaned on my experience to realized that fostering open communication was the key to success. Midway in the project, IT was focused on system features, while sales and customer service teams were more concerned about usability and workflow disruptions. To bridge this gap, I established regular feedback sessions and open forums, allowing departments to voice their concerns and expectations. By actively understanding their needs, we customized the CRM to align with their daily operations, ensuring it streamlined processes rather than complicating them. Additionally, *I broke down silos by bringing together IT, sales, marketing, and customer support teams in the planning phase, fostering collaboration and shared ownership*. As a result, adoption rates increased, resistance decreased, and the CRM became a valuable business tool that improved customer engagement and operational efficiency. This experience reinforced that *technology implementations succeed not when IT dictates solutions, but when cross-functional teams build them together*.

Lesson 5: Prioritize Security Without Stifling Innovation

Balancing the need for security with the pursuit of innovation is a constant challenge. Effective IT executives manage this balance by **embedding security into the culture** without hindering creativity.

Key Takeaways:

1. **Adopt a Proactive Security Posture**: Regularly assess risks, update protocols, and implement robust safeguards.
2. **Educate Employees**: Provide training on cybersecurity best practices to reduce human error.
3. **Enable Secure Innovation**: Design systems and processes that allow experimentation while protecting sensitive data.

My experience, where I applied it and how I learned this valuable lesson:

During a global cloud migration project, I learned firsthand the importance of adopting a proactive security posture. Early in the transition, a routine risk assessment uncovered vulnerability in access controls, prompting us to strengthen authentication protocols and implement real-time threat monitoring before they could be exploited. However, security isn't just about technology—it's also about people. A phishing attempt targeting a senior executive reinforced the need to educate employees, so we launched company-wide cybersecurity awareness training, reducing security incidents by 40%. At the same time, we ensured that security didn't become a barrier to innovation. By enabling secure innovation, we designed a zero-trust architecture and automated compliance checks, allowing teams to experiment with AI-driven analytics while protecting sensitive data. This experience proved that *cybersecurity is not just an IT responsibility—it's a business imperative that must be embedded in culture, process, and technology*.

Lesson 6: The Importance of Continuous Learning

Technology evolves rapidly, and staying relevant requires a commitment to ongoing education. Effective IT leaders prioritize both their own development and that of their teams. *Learn and do not be afraid of failure!*

Key Takeaways:

1. **Stay Curious**: Continuously explore emerging trends and technologies to stay ahead of the curve.
2. **Invest in Training**: Provide opportunities for your team to acquire new skills and certifications.
3. **Learn from Failure**: Treat mistakes as learning opportunities and encourage a culture of resilience.

My experience, where I applied it and how I learned this valuable lesson:

During the implementation of a new AI-driven analytics platform, I quickly realized *the importance of staying curious and continuously exploring emerging technologies*. Initially, we faced resistance due to a lack of in-house expertise, which highlighted the need to invest in training. To address this, we launched a structured upskilling program, enabling our teams to gain AI and machine learning certifications, which not only improved adoption but also boosted innovation. We created champions in the organization. Despite our best efforts, the first rollout had unexpected data integration issues, causing delays. Instead of placing blame, we treated it as a learning opportunity—conducting a post-mortem, refining our approach, and fostering a culture of resilience. The result? A second, more successful deployment that enhanced predictive insights and drove smarter decision-making across the organization. This experience reinforced that true innovation comes from curiosity, continuous learning, and the courage to turn failures into future successes.

Lesson 7: Measure and Communicate Impact

In IT, if you can't prove the value, you might as well be pitching vaporware. Executives don't want to hear about server uptimes or microservices—they want to know how it boosts revenue, cuts costs, or keeps customers happy. That's why the best IT leaders don't just present data; they tell compelling stories.

Want buy-in for a new automation tool? Don't just say it will "streamline workflows"—show how it will save 500 hours a month, reduce errors by 40%, and let teams focus on high-value work instead of chasing spreadsheets. The secret? Speak in outcomes, not just outputs. *When stakeholders see IT as a business enabler rather than an expense, support follows naturally.* Because at the end of the day, the best way to sell an idea isn't through slides full of stats—it's through stories that make the impact impossible to ignore.

Key Takeaways:

1. **Define Clear Metrics**: Establish KPIs that align with business goals and measure progress consistently.
2. **Tell Compelling Stories**: Use data and real-world examples to illustrate the impact of technology investments.
3. **Engage Stakeholders Regularly**: Keep stakeholders informed through updates, reports, and presentations.

My experience, where I applied it and how I learned this valuable lesson:

This is one of my most important lessons. During a company-wide digital transformation initiative, I quickly realized that without clear metrics, it was difficult to demonstrate the true impact of our efforts. To address this, we defined KPIs that aligned with business goals—tracking operational efficiency, cost savings, and customer satisfaction improvements. However, raw data alone wasn't enough to gain executive buy-in. I learned the power of telling compelling stories by translating metrics into real-world business impact, such as how automation reduced processing times by 50%, or how errors in Order management improved revenue and profits or how AI-driven insights cut customer churn by 20%. Regular engagement with stakeholders was also critical; by providing concise updates, interactive dashboards, and strategic presentations, we kept leadership aligned and secured continued investment in the initiative. This experience reinforced that *success isn't just about delivering results—it's about effectively communicating those results to drive momentum and long-term support.*

Lesson 8: Foster a Resilient and Inclusive Culture

In IT (and in life), resilience isn't just about bouncing back—it's about bouncing forward. And the best way to future-proof a team? Diversity and inclusion. A team that brings different perspectives, backgrounds, and experiences to the table isn't just nice to have—it's a business advantage.

When challenges hit (because they always do), an adaptable, diverse team won't crumble—they'll pivot, innovate, and find solutions others wouldn't have considered. Whether it's a cybersecurity breach, a failed product launch, or an unexpected market shift, the teams that thrive are built to handle uncertainty with confidence. Because in a world where change is the only constant, a one-size-fits-all mindset is a one-way ticket to irrelevance.

Key Takeaways:

1. **Promote Diversity**: Build teams with diverse backgrounds, experiences, and perspectives.
2. **Encourage Resilience**: Support employees through challenges and provide resources for mental and emotional well-being.
3. **Lead by Example**: Demonstrate inclusive leadership practices that create a sense of belonging for everyone.

My experience, where I applied it and how I learned this valuable lesson:

Early in my career, I made the classic mistake of hiring a team that thought just like me—big on tech, light on perspective. The result? A brilliantly efficient, yet painfully one-dimensional approach to problem-solving. I quickly learned that promoting diversity isn't just a corporate buzzword, it is the secret sauce to innovation. So, I started bringing in people with diverse backgrounds, industries, and ways of thinking. At first, meetings felt like a chaotic brainstorming session at a coffee shop, but soon, fresh ideas and creative solutions emerged. Of course, diversity also meant encouraging resilience—supporting team members through challenges, not just projects. I prioritized open dialogue, mental health resources, and a culture where mistakes were learning opportunities, not career killers. Most importantly, I had to lead by example—actively listening, adapting, and ensuring every voice was heard. The result? A high-performing team that tackled challenges from every angle—and, ironically, made me realize just how much I still had to learn!

Conclusion: At this point in my learning/ leading journey...

The IT Executive Playbook: Less Ctrl+Alt+Delete, More Shift+Lead+Innovate.

Being an IT executive is a bit like upgrading a mission-critical system while it's still running—demanding, occasionally chaotic, but ultimately rewarding when everything clicks. The secret? People first, tech second, business always.

By aligning technology with business strategy, embracing change like a pro, and making collaboration your secret weapon, *you will not just keep the lights on—you will illuminate the path forward.* These lessons are not just battle scars from years in the trenches; they are a blueprint for leading with impact, resilience, and just the right amount of audacity.

Leading effectively as an IT executive is not just about technical expertise, it's about vision, adaptability, and the ability to inspire and empower those around you.

Technology will continue to evolve at an unprecedented pace, and with it, the role of IT leadership will expand and transform. The most effective leaders are those who embrace change, remain lifelong learners, and continuously refine their ability to communicate, collaborate, and drive meaningful progress.

As you move forward in your own leadership journey, remember that success is not defined solely by technical achievements or business outcomes—it is measured by the impact you have on your teams, the growth you inspire in others, and the legacy you leave behind. The lessons shared in this chapter are not rigid rules, but guiding principles meant to be adapted to your unique experiences and challenges.

Leadership is a journey, not a destination. Stay curious, stay resilient, and lead with purpose. The future of IT—and the success of the organizations we serve—depends on leaders who are willing to step up, make tough decisions, and drive transformation with integrity and vision.

ABOUT THE AUTHOR

Kamal Mohanty

Kamal Mohanty is a seasoned IT executive known for his expertise in driving digital transformation and cloud strategy across global organizations. With over 25 years of experience, most recently as Sr. VP of IT at Miller Zell Inc. in Atlanta, he has a passion for leveraging emerging technologies to solve complex business challenges. Kamal has deep experience in cloud migrations, DevOps, enterprise architecture, and AI-driven solutions, and is recognized for his ability to align technology with business objectives.

His key strengths include strategic vision, cross-functional collaboration, and a commitment to continuous improvement. Kamal strives for innovation that drives efficiency and empowers teams to exceed expectations in today's rapidly evolving digital landscape.

When not working Kamal enjoys playing sports, cricket, tennis, soccer—and spending time with his family on food adventures and travels. He enjoys classical and contemporary Indian music. Kamal is also big student of various Defense technologies.

Being an IT executive is a bit like upgrading a mission-critical system while it's still running—demanding, occasionally chaotic, but ultimately rewarding when everything clicks. The secret? People first, tech second, business always.

When I Discovered Me

Dorothy Parks

How many times in your youth were you asked or did you ask yourself, "What do you want to be when you grow up?" I remember countless times when I considered my future career and everything that might lie ahead. Little did I know just how many options were truly available to me.

Growing up in an upper middle-class family, I was only exposed to a narrow circle of individuals and professionals who were carefully selected by my parents. I attended private schools through the 10th grade, until I begged my mother and father to let me enroll in a new public high school nearby. They eventually agreed.

What a different world I encountered. Teachers wore regular clothes instead of habits, and students came from diverse cultures and backgrounds. Gone were the navy-blue pleated skirts, embroidered jackets, white blouses, and black penny loafers. Suddenly, I was free to choose my own clothes and shoes. I wore things I actually liked and that felt fashionable. I formed friendships with girls and boys from all walks of life. It felt like I had entered the real world. I was off and running, embracing new experiences and life's many challenges.

Graduating from high school with honors, I set off for college without a clear idea of what professional path I would pursue. My mother, a dedicated educator, insisted I follow in her footsteps and work toward a master's and eventually a PhD. I still remember her saying, "Education is an excellent field that you should embark on, tackle, and achieve."

But, being a bit defiant and determined to forge my own way, I resisted the idea of stepping into the same career she had chosen.

At that time, the conversations happening around me centered on a familiar set of professions: doctors, nurses, teachers, secretaries, lawyers, accountants, and entrepreneurs. No one ever mentioned the thousands of other careers that existed beyond that short list. With such a narrow view of what was possible, and a strong natural ability in math and numbers, I eventually declared Finance as my major in my sophomore year. I excelled in the subject and felt confident I had found my place.

By the middle of my junior year, I landed an internship with a state-sponsored organization. On my first day, I was greeted by a senior leader who introduced himself and casually asked about my studies. I was clear he wasn't truly listening. He shuffled papers on his desk and never once made eye contact. Toward the end of our brief exchange, he looked up and said, "Okay, let's get you started. How many words can you type per minute?"

I must have looked completely perplexed and more than a little annoyed. Without much thought, I shot back, "Eighty words per minute, but I'm not here to type or file. I'm seeking a professional internship where I can apply my financial knowledge. If that's not what this is, I'll speak with my counselor."

He seemed stunned, either by my response, my tone, or maybe both.

As I walked out of his office, I thought to myself: *Is this what I'm in for? A career where people don't see you, don't respect you, and just assume you're there for a basic job?* I could wash cars or bag groceries without a degree if that's all the world expects of me.

After consulting with my counselor, I was told the issue had been addressed and was asked that I return to the same organization the following week.

This time, I was greeted by the Chief Financial Officer, who welcomed me warmly as we walked to his office. He apologized for the earlier experience and took a genuine interest in our conversation. He explained that he had reviewed my transcript, was impressed by my academic performance, and wanted to place me in the financial office for a summer program. He described the work I'd be doing and wished me success in the role.

I was thrilled. The internship gave me hands-on experience in nearly every facet of accounting, from number crunching to payroll to financial reporting. When my 16-week assignment ended, I sat down for an exit interview with the CFO, who shared that he had received glowing feedback from multiple departments about my performance.

He told me that if I was interested, he'd like me to consider returning after graduation to take a full-time position within his organization. Naturally, I was over the moon—but I took his offer as more of an encouraging gesture than a real opportunity. Still, his words gave me a powerful boost of confidence at a pivotal moment in my journey.

Who Am I? How Did I Become Me? What Lessons Did I Learn Along the Way? Part 2

I'm someone who values self-respect and understands the importance of clear, direct communication. Early in my career, I made it a priority to set professional boundaries and learned that being assertive often leads to positive outcomes. My approach to work has always been shaped by a commitment to align each role with my personal goals, while remaining adaptable and open to new ideas. Most importantly, I've learned to prioritize professional relationships built on mutual respect—because those connections are essential for growth and long-term success in any organization.

The next year, after completing my college coursework and graduating with honors once again, I took a three-month sabbatical before stepping into the next stage of life: job hunting. I applied for several positions at banks and corporate companies, mostly roles in finance and accounting. But despite my efforts, I wasn't having much success. Time after time, I heard the same feedback: "Your academic record and resume are outstanding, but you're overqualified for this position." Eventually, I realized that was just a polite rejection line.

Feeling discouraged and a bit sorry for myself, I began to wonder if my mother had been right all along. Maybe I *should* have chosen a career in education. But then, the lightbulb went off. I'd already been offered a potential opportunity by the organization where I completed my internship. *Call them,* I told myself.

The next week, I picked up the phone and spoke with the CFO. He remembered me immediately and my work during the internship. He told me a position had just opened and invited me to come in. The very next day, I was up early, dressed in my best business attire, and ready to take on the world (or at least a small piece of it).

When I arrived, I met with the HR director, who described the opportunity. To my amazement, I was speechless. The role being offered was an entry-level management position overseeing a brand-new operation. *Was I dreaming?* Someone pinch me. After a moment to gather my composure, I started asking questions. I accepted the challenge, feeling terror and exhilaration all at once. *How did this happen?*

Who Am I? How Did I Become Me? What Lessons Did I Learn Along the Way? Part 3

I am someone who embodies perseverance, resilience, and proactive decision-making. Despite facing early rejections and moments of self-doubt, I refused to give up. Instead, I took the initiative to reconnect with the organization where I had interned. That decision uncovered an unexpected and rewarding opportunity. This experience reaffirmed the value of staying positive and proactive in the face of setbacks. I also came to understand the importance of leveraging past relationships and keeping doors open. Sometimes, the right opportunity appears when you least expect it, and with the right mindset and initiative, those moments can lead to meaningful career breakthroughs.

After spending more than two years in this management role, a friend invited me to lunch one day. When I arrived at the restaurant, she was joined by one of her associates—the HR director at a large engineering firm. After some friendly conversation about work and a few shared personal interests, the HR director asked if I had ever considered exploring other opportunities. I told him honestly that I hadn't; I was fully engaged in my current role and hadn't thought about making a change.

He went on to explain that his company needed someone with my skills and leadership experience to help strengthen their management team. He asked if I would be open to a conversation about potential opportunities. Since the company was located just a block away from my office, setting up a meeting was easy. Not long after, I met with him again and spoke with several of the firm's executives. As I was leaving, he let me know they would be in touch soon.

The following week, I returned to my office to find a message from him asking for both personal and professional references. A week later, I received a formal job offer. While I was honored and intrigued, I was also hesitant to leave a company that had treated me so well. I gave serious thought to what the new role could offer in terms of growth and career advancement. In the end, I challenged myself to take the leap, embrace the opportunity, and aim higher. I accepted the position, which involved co-managing the Finance, Accounting, and IT departments. From there, I moved quickly up the ladder, first to Manager, then Director, and finally to CFO, all while attending night school to earn my master's degree and CPA certification.

Who Am I? How Did I Become Me? What Lessons Did I Learn Along the Way? Part 4

I am someone who embraces new opportunities and understands the importance of stepping outside my comfort zone, even when I feel content in my current role. Although I was satisfied with my job, I chose to explore new possibilities when they arose, which resulted in meaningful career advancement and personal growth. I recognized the importance of considering long-term benefits and wasn't afraid to make bold decisions in pursuit of progress. Dedicated to continuous improvement, I pursued additional education and professional certifications while continuing to grow in my career. This approach reflects my belief that seeking growth and taking calculated risks often leads to valuable rewards.

Performing in these roles, I quickly discovered that acceptance as a female executive was extremely rare. It was largely a man's world, filled with ego and politics. One aspect of my responsibilities was handling and investing millions of dollars each day with our banking institution. After placing investments by phone for several years, one day the chief investment banker asked if he and some of his colleagues could come out to meet the CFO in person. My assistant confirmed and scheduled the meeting.

On the day of their visit, I was tied up with an issue in the payroll department, so my assistant escorted them into my office to wait. About 10 minutes later, I returned and greeted them. One of the bankers responded that they were there to meet the CFO and would wait. I took a seat behind my desk and said again, "Hello, I'm Ms. Parks, the CFO." I wish I had a camera with me. Their eyes widened, and jaws dropped as if to say, "You can't be the person we deal with every day who's managing millions of dollars." A few moments passed before they regained their composure and we were able to proceed with the meeting.

This was just one of many moments where I faced challenges of acceptance, especially as a young Black woman in such a high-ranking position. Despite the obvious prejudices, I never allowed people's actions or ignorance to defeat or discourage me.

Who Am I? How Did I Become Me? What Lessons Did I Learn Along the Way? Part 5

I am a person who is resilient, self-confident, and determined. I have successfully navigated the challenges of prejudice and societal expectations. As a young Black female executive in a male-dominated industry, I faced bias but stayed focused, continuing to perform at a high level despite external challenges. I understand the importance of not letting others' ignorance or assumptions define my worth or capabilities. By maintaining professionalism and inner confidence, I have achieved personal growth and success, even when others initially doubted or underestimated me.

About eight years passed, and with all the experience I had gained at the engineering firm, I had the bold idea to change direction and step into entrepreneurship. I launched my own financial consulting company, offering accounting services and financial guidance to small and midsize businesses. I took on the role of CEO. Naturally, working for yourself brings a completely different level of dedication and responsibility. While I felt a deep sense of pride and accomplishment, I also faced the constant challenge of marketing my company, showcasing my skills, and growing my client base. After about a year of building a sustainable business with a steady income, I partnered with a colleague to open a computer company that sold mid-size computers and financial software tailored to small and midsize businesses.

The logic behind investing in both areas of business was to capture a specific segment of clients who needed both a reliable financial system and expert consultation. By offering products and services together, we aimed to provide a complete solution for managing financial operations. While we reached a portion of our intended market, we struggled to compete with larger players like the newly opened Computer World and IBM. Looking back, we realized we had missed the mark by not conducting enough market research. Eventually, we dissolved the partnership and closed the computer business.

Who Am I? How Did I Become Me? What Lessons Did I Learn Along the Way? Part 6

I was an entrepreneur who valued careful planning, market research, and strategic decision-making. While I took great pride in building a successful financial consulting company, my experience with a failed computer business taught me an important lesson about the necessity of thorough market analysis before launching a new venture. I've learned that even with a strong idea and unwavering dedication, business success depends on understanding the competition, identifying market needs, and making well-informed decisions. I also embrace adaptability and know when it is time to pivot or close a business when it becomes clear that the venture is no longer viable.

While continuing to operate my financial consulting business, I secured an assignment with a privately held hotel company that needed financial support. After working closely with the CFO for over a year, I was invited to consider taking on a major leadership role within the company. I took time to think through the offer, weighing the potential to transform operations and the financial benefits that came with the position. In the end, I accepted the opportunity.

Through strong execution, performance, and leadership, my responsibilities quickly grew. I soon found myself managing both the financial operations and Information Technology teams. When the company prepared for a corporate IPO and underwent a significant reorganization, I saw it as another opportunity to grow, even though I had no prior experience in this area. I wasn't afraid to step up and immerse myself in learning everything I could.

Following the IPO, now under a new corporate name, the company expanded rapidly, and mergers and acquisitions began accelerating. I became a member of the acquisition team and traveled across the U.S. and Europe, conducting due diligence on targeted companies. This was yet another learning experience. My performance on these assignments led me once more to an advancement in positions.

At this point, I found myself not only leading the finance and information technology departments but also traveling the globe to pursue business acquisitions that would expand our company's portfolio. On one of those trips, during a visit to India, I hit a wall of complete exhaustion. It was then that I realized, despite my passion for the work and my constant drive to learn and achieve, it was time to reassess and streamline my focus. I needed to make a choice: continue down the path of finance or fully commit to technology.

This was not an easy decision. I enjoyed both areas immensely. Numbers were familiar and predictable, two plus two would always equal four. But the world of technology was dynamic, evolving every single day. After much reflection, I made my choice: IT would be my path forward. Since then, the experiences I've had in this field have been challenging, energizing, and deeply fulfilling. Technology continues to spark my curiosity and has held my interest like nothing else.

Who Am I? How Did I Become Me? What Lessons Did I Learn Along the Way? Part 7

I am a person who embraces growth opportunities and values continuous learning. I have a strong will to take on new challenges, even without prior experience, and that mindset has fueled significant professional growth and accomplishment. My adaptability and leadership have enabled me to play a key role in major corporate transformations. I also understand the importance of self-reflection and the courage it takes to make tough decisions, particularly when faced with competing interests. Ultimately, I chose a path that aligned with my personal passions and long-term fulfillment. Despite having a solid foundation in finance, I shifted my focus to technology, a field that excites and motivates me. This decision reflects my belief in following what sparks joy and engagement as a path to lasting success and satisfaction.

In 2012, while working in my office in New York, I received devastating news about my family in Atlanta. My immediate reaction was to get there as quickly as possible to be with them. Once I arrived, I realized the situation was far more serious than I had anticipated. I found myself at another crossroad in life. My family needed me in Atlanta, and I couldn't walk away from them, but I also loved my job in New York and understood how important my responsibilities were to the company. Still, I only have one family. My internal priorities came into sharp focus, and a voice in my head said, "Come on, Dorothy, you know the answer." And I did. But knowing it didn't make the next phone call any easier.

I made the difficult decision to resign from my position and, with deep conviction, turned my focus to supporting my family in Atlanta. Within a month, I received a phone call from the CEO of one of my major vendor firms based in Boca Raton, Florida. He had heard about my departure and asked whether I would be interested in becoming their District President and Chief Information Officer for the Southern region. Accepting the position allowed me to remain local to Atlanta, limit travel to within the region, and continue my career through an exciting new venture. It also gave me the chance to meet phenomenal people, join several industry organizations, and volunteer on various boards.

Who Am I? How Did I Become Me? What Lessons Did I Learn Along the Way? Part 8

I am a person who understands the importance of prioritizing what truly matters in life: family, personal values, and well-being. When faced with the difficult choice between continuing my career or supporting my loved ones during a critical time, I chose to be there for my family. Though it was not an easy decision, it ultimately led to an unexpected opportunity that allowed me to remain close to home while continuing to grow professionally. My experience shows that aligning decisions with personal priorities, even in times of uncertainty, can result in deeply rewarding outcomes. Staying open to change can lead to new and fulfilling paths.

One Friday evening in April of 2016, I had the pleasure of having dinner with an associate who worked for a large NASA research organization. He was developing a summer flight academy program for students ages 16 to 22 and wanted my support. One component of the academy focused on the use and evolution of technology in the aerospace industry. I was asked to co-chair the program, and I saw it as a wonderful opportunity to mentor, contribute, and give back to my community and the younger generation.

During dinner that evening, one of my associate's friends stopped by and joined us. As we talked, he became intrigued by my career background and asked if I would be willing to share my resume. He mentioned that Gwinnett County could benefit from someone with my experience. About a week later, he followed up with an email requesting my resume. I sent it, somewhat reluctantly, and didn't give it much more thought.

In February of 2017, while working from my home office, I received a call from Gwinnett County asking if I would be willing to meet with one of their executives to discuss a potential employment opportunity. With my professional instincts always sharp, I knew it was wise never to miss a chance to hear someone out, so I agreed to the meeting. About two weeks after that initial conversation, I received a second call requesting another meeting to gather more details about my career background. A month later, the third call came, this time asking if I could meet with the County Administrator.

At that point, I was starting to grow weary of the back-and-forth and felt the need to refocus on my current business. Still, I reminded myself that you never know where a path might lead, even one you didn't seek out. I attended the meeting, and to my surprise, the County Administrator greeted me with, "Dorothy, I'm so glad you'll be joining us here at the County. Your background is astonishing, and I know you'll bring great value to our organization." Not wanting to appear stunned, I smiled, shook his hand, and nodded in quiet acceptance.

Now, nearly nine years later, I proudly serve as the Chief Information Officer of Technology Services for Gwinnett County Government. Gwinnett is the most ethnically diverse county in Georgia, with large populations of Black, Hispanic, and Asian residents. It is also the fastest-growing county in the state, home to more than one million people.

Who Am I? How Did I Become Me? What Lessons Did I Learn Along the Way? Part 9

I am someone who remains open to unexpected opportunities and values the power of networking, even in casual or informal settings. What began as a simple dinner conversation led to a meaningful career shift, all because I chose to share my resume without overthinking it. That small action opened the door to a valuable opportunity with Gwinnett County. This experience reinforced my belief that chance encounters can lead to significant outcomes. It also reminded me of the importance of being approachable, staying willing to support others, and remaining receptive to new possibilities. Sometimes, the most rewarding opportunities come from places we least expect.

So, in summary, Who Am I? How Did I Become Me? What Lessons Did I Learn Along the Way?

Ultimately, I am a person shaped by my experiences, values, and the many people I've encountered throughout my life. My journey has been a blend of challenges, growth, and self-discovery, each moment contributing to the person I am today. I became who

I am through a series of personal and external influences—family, education, work, relationships, and the trials I've faced along the way.

Each chapter has taught me something: the importance of resilience, the power of kindness, and the value of self-reflection. I've learned that mistakes are not failures, but opportunities to grow. Embracing change, rather than resisting it, has been key to evolving over time. Above all, I've come to understand that becoming my true self means accepting both my strengths and my flaws, while always striving to grow.

ABOUT THE AUTHOR

Dorothy Parks

Dorothy Parks is a seasoned Information Technology Executive with over 30 years of leadership experience in the technology industry. She currently serves as Chief Information Officer and Director of Information Technology Services for Gwinnett County Government, where she drives the strategic alignment of technology initiatives with organizational goals in a dynamic, fast-paced environment.

Dorothy is recognized for her ability to lead high-performing teams, implement robust IT systems, and maximize operational efficiency. Her leadership encompasses enterprise-level technology strategy, systems implementation, cybersecurity, and regulatory compliance. A results-driven professional, she has consistently delivered innovative solutions that enhance service delivery and support business transformation.

Before joining Gwinnett County in 2017, Dorothy held several executive roles, including Division President and CIO at Atlantic Partners Corporation, and CEO and Managing Partner at DAP Services, LLC. She has also served as Vice President of Strategic Initiatives and Global Applications at Wyndham Worldwide, and held senior leadership roles at Cendant Corporation, Hospitality Franchise Systems, and Days Inn of America. Earlier in her career, she was CFO at Parsons Brinckerhoff/Tudor Engineering.

Dorothy holds degrees in Management, Economics, and Finance from Clark Atlanta University and is certified in ITIL, Six Sigma, Project Management, and is a Certified Public Accountant (CPA). She is an active member of several professional organizations including the CIO Forum, Women in Technology, and the Technology Association of Georgia.

A respected speaker and advocate for lifelong learning, Dorothy is committed to driving innovation, integrity, and business growth through transformative technology leadership.

When Seeking a Position in Management

Gary Wilde

If you're hoping to move into a management role but have never held a formal leadership position before, you're not alone—and you're not out of the running. While transitioning from a technical or individual contributor role into management can feel like a leap, it's absolutely achievable with the right preparation, mindset, and strategy.

Clarifying Your Motivation and Understanding the Role

When you're aiming for a management role, it's important to reflect on your motivations. Doing so can help you avoid the pitfalls of misaligning your aspirations with the realities of managing people.

Some common motivations for wanting to move into management include:

- Earning a higher salary
- Gaining a job title that commands more respect
- Receiving recognition for your capabilities and talent
- Expanding your skill set beyond your current area of expertise
- Advancing your career

While there's nothing wrong with any of these motivations, only the last two involve thinking about the actual skills required to succeed as a people manager.

Being effective in a management role requires a broad range of skills, including:

- Deep subject matter expertise
- Strong interpersonal (people) skills
- Financial literacy
- Business acumen
- A solid understanding of organizational policies and processes

Building the Right Skills for Leadership

Aspiring people managers often already have strong subject matter expertise, developed through continuous education—such as attending conferences, engaging with professional associations, earning professional credentials, and staying current on industry trends and innovations.

The other essential management skills can be learned. Start by taking leadership or people skills courses that cover the fundamentals, such as:

- Time management
- Navigating difficult conversations
- Negotiation and delegation
- Creating effective presentations
- Giving and receiving feedback
- Problem-solving and decision-making
- Root cause analysis
- Growing emotional intelligence

It's also helpful to build a foundation in business skills. An introductory course in accounting and financial literacy can teach you how to read financial statements. From there, connect with your finance department to learn about your organization's budgeting process and how leaders manage both operating and capital budgets.

Business acumen and organizational savvy come from understanding how your organization operates—its key processes, policies, and the roles of each department. Start by exploring your organization's intranet and external website. Review the company's values and strategic plan, and take time to understand the reasoning behind them. Why were those particular goals and priorities chosen?

In short, work to develop a strong grasp of your organization's business model and culture. One effective way to do this is by following the company's social media channels. These can offer insight into what senior leadership values, and what matters to them will matter to anyone in a management role.

Be clear about the type of management position you're aiming for. What are your personal career goals, and which kind of role best aligns with them? Pay attention to what topics capture your interest. What do you think about, read, or watch in your spare time? These can offer valuable clues about your true aspirations. For example, if your background is in road engineering, it's unlikely you'd be pursuing a management role in dentistry or emergency medical services.

Know Your Organization and Speak Its Language

Once you've identified the position(s) you're interested in, carefully read the job description and start working toward meeting as many of the minimum qualifications as possible. That may include specific education or experience requirements. Go a step further by talking with people who are currently in that role. They can provide real-world insights into what the job actually involves and which skills are most important for success. While a job posting may list dozens of responsibilities, someone in the role can tell you which of those truly matter day to day, and what it took for them to build those skills.

Next, put yourself in the shoes of a hiring manager. What kinds of questions might they ask during an interview for that role? Use those as a guide to prepare and strengthen your readiness.

Research the leadership values your organization emphasizes. Then, identify real-world examples from your own experience that demonstrate how you've embodied those values—even if you haven't held a formal leadership role yet. These examples will be especially important if you're invited to interview for a management position. A common mistake among first-time management candidates is showing up unprepared to answer questions about leadership and people skills. Don't let that be you.

Also, make your ambitions known. Opportunities are unlikely to come your way unless others know you're seeking them. One of the best examples from my own experience was when I had the courage to tell my Director that I was looking for a growth opportunity. At the time, I was in a great job, managing a team I loved working with. It suited my strengths and gave me chances to speak at both provincial and national conferences because of the innovative work my team was doing. But deep down, I knew I had more to offer and needed a new outlet for that potential. The following week, I had a Commissioner visit my desk and invite me to his office for a chat, and two weeks after that, I had moved into a new role that paved the way for the next steps of my evolution and career. This could not have happened if I hadn't had the courage to make my ambitions and aspirations known. Doors will not open for you if people don't know you want them opened.

So…who should you talk to about your goals?

Position Yourself as a Leader Before You Have the Title

You also want others to see you as management material. That means consistently conducting yourself with integrity and being perceived as ethical, honest, and dependable. If you have a reputation for shady behaviour, word will get around, and you won't be trusted. The same goes for staying silent about important issues to avoid looking bad or for betraying confidences. Instead, aim to be transparent and proactive when problems arise. Speak up early, and strive to be seen as a trusted problem-solver.

One of the best books I've read on this topic is *The Speed of Trust* by Stephen Covey. It offers valuable insights into how trust is built and lost, and the consequences of both.

Even better, seek out anonymous, real-world feedback from people you've worked with—both peers and supervisors—by requesting a 360-degree assessment. I've done this many times throughout my career and always found it incredibly valuable. These assessments can reveal patterns in your behaviour, tendencies, and reputation that are hard to uncover otherwise.

The right mindset is to treat this feedback as precious insight. Use it to deepen your self-awareness, play to your strengths, and shore up any critical weaknesses. You'll always get more return from your efforts when you lean into your natural talents, rather than trying to improve every area of weakness. That said, it *is* important to address any critical weaknesses that could seriously undermine your career.

Another key part of presenting yourself as a professional is having a polished, up-to-date resume. Ask a trusted friend, advisor, or mentor to review it and give honest feedback. Keep in mind that resumes are not one-size-fits-all. You'll need to tailor yours for each job you apply to, highlighting the strengths and experiences that best align with the specific requirements of the posting. This significantly increases your chances of landing an interview.

Acting with integrity also means being accountable and encouraging accountability in others. If you commit to completing something by a certain date, do you follow through, or do you tend to offer excuses? High-performing teams thrive when every member is willing to take responsibility for their own commitments and to respectfully hold others to theirs as well. When just one team member misses a deadline, it can create a ripple effect—delaying others, increasing workloads, and sometimes forcing colleagues to work overtime or give up weekends. A great way to prepare for a job interview is to gather concrete examples of how you've held yourself and others accountable in a respectful and constructive way.

One meaningful way to shift how your colleagues perceive you is to mentor a more junior team member. When you take the initiative to support someone else's growth, others begin to see you as a leader—someone who contributes to building up others and to broader organizational goals and not just your own advancement. Another good way to build your reputation is by understanding what matters most to senior leadership, including their values, and aligning your behaviour accordingly.

One thing that helped me early in my career was realizing that senior leadership often speaks a different 'language' than front-line staff. Each group focuses on what's most relevant to their role. Front-line employees usually talk about daily tasks, internal processes, coworkers, and client needs. Senior leaders, on the other hand, focus on profit and loss, strategic goals, business outcomes, and employee engagement and enablement.

If you want to connect with management and have management see you as a future leader, begin framing your contributions in ways that align with their priorities. The more you speak their language, the more relatable and capable you'll appear in their eyes.

Expand Your Visibility and Your Value

Seeking out a mentor is a smart and effective strategy if you're working toward a management position. I've had mentors throughout most of my career, and have benefited considerably from that. I've also returned the favour by mentoring others along the way. Mentors can—and often should—change depending on where you are in your career, offering different perspectives and guidance as your goals and understanding evolve.

Unfortunately, some people never seek out mentors. Sometimes it's pride—a lack of humility. Other times it's fear—worrying that a more senior person might reject the request. If you're feeling hesitant, consider asking a trusted colleague to help make the introduction or gauge the potential mentor's interest on your behalf. In my experience, when you approach someone with respect and humility, they will almost always be willing to help. Some organizations even have formal mentorship programs to connect mentors and mentees, making the process easier. Don't let hesitation hold you back. There are simply too many advantages to having a mentor—learning from their experience, gaining insight, and receiving support that can help you grow and succeed in your career.

Another key to positioning yourself for management is demonstrating your value through results. You build credibility with leadership when you consistently deliver outcomes and earn a reputation for follow-through. In fact, delivering results isn't optional for people managers—it's essential. If you can't deliver meaningful results, your time in a leadership role will likely be short.

This also requires a shift in mindset. It's not just about working hard or being seen as busy; it's about achieving results that align with your organization's strategic goals, not just your personal interests. Ideally, you can quantify those results—such as reducing operational costs, lowering accident rates, or improving team performance.

People-related results can be trickier to measure, but they still matter. Metrics like employee engagement survey results or tracking a decrease in complaints escalated to senior leadership can offer concrete evidence of your leadership impact.

Show Initiative

Building a strong reputation also means showing initiative. This signals to others that you're ready for more responsibility. Initiative can take many forms: proposing a process improvement, identifying a new business opportunity, suggesting a health and safety enhancement, or stepping up to help a colleague. It might mean volunteering to join a project team, especially on high-priority or strategic initiatives. You could also offer to chair a meeting, prepare presentation materials, or do background research.

Don't worry if you're not ready to lead an entire large-scale project. What's more realistic, and just as valuable, is contributing to smaller parts of a project or taking the lead on specific work packages. These experiences help build trust, and if you deliver well, management will remember. The next time an opportunity arises, they may come to you with greater responsibilities—possibly even a leadership role.

Another powerful way to show initiative is by bringing forward thoughtful proposals to senior leadership. Don't be afraid to speak up when you see an opportunity that could benefit the organization. Early in my career as a young engineer, I approached the CEO of Westinghouse's Turbine and Generator division in Hamilton, Ontario, with a proposal to expand the company's services into North Africa. I had just finished a two-year project in that area, working on the construction and commissioning of a major power plant—part of what was then the largest civil engineering project in the world. The CEO invited me to lunch to discuss the idea. Although the proposal didn't move forward, the conversation made a lasting impression.

In another role within the automotive industry, a mechanical engineer colleague and I collaborated on a patent application, which we successfully submitted. That too drew positive attention from senior management. Even if these initiatives don't always lead to immediate outcomes, they show that you're engaged, forward-thinking, and willing to contribute beyond your job description.

Build Your Personal and Professional Networks

Another way to strengthen your path to management is by actively building your personal network. It's much easier to get things done when you can simply pick up the phone and call someone you know, rather than trying to navigate unfamiliar processes or cold-contacting colleagues. Having a strong internal network helps build your reputation as someone who gets things done—and these same connections may even serve as advocates during the interview process for a management role.

Focus on building relationships not just with peers, but also with decision-makers and leaders within your organization. And don't forget to grow your external network as well. Cultivating relationships with regulators, strategic partners, suppliers, and others outside your organization demonstrates strong people and business skills. Attending conferences, industry events, and association meetings are all great ways to make those connections and showcase your leadership potential.

Strategize Your Path to Management

A continuous learning mindset, along with flexibility and resilience, are essential leadership qualities, especially in today's rapidly changing world. Employees who are seen as unwilling to adapt, who fall behind in their knowledge and skills, or who give up easily in the face of challenges are unlikely to be considered for management roles. Cultural competence is also increasingly important. In our diverse workplaces, being seen as culturally unaware or insensitive can significantly limit your opportunities.

One of the best resources I've found on organizational culture is *Myth, Magic, Mindset* by John O. Burdett. It shaped much of my understanding of how culture is created, measured, and evolved within organizations. This aligns with something I mentioned earlier—the importance of developing a deep understanding of your organization's culture and how it does business.

When you're looking to move into a management role for the first time, the best opportunities often exist within your current organization. That's where your reputation is already established and people already know your capabilities. When you apply externally, you're starting from scratch, and hiring managers may struggle to gauge your trustworthiness and potential. That said, there are definitely times when applying externally is necessary—for instance, if there are no promotion opportunities in your area of interest, or if the role you want simply doesn't exist within your current organization.

One common frustration I've heard from staff—and experienced myself—is when job postings require prior management experience. It can feel like a catch-22: how do you gain that experience if no one will give you the opportunity? The best approach is to apply the strategies laid out in this article. Building your competencies, developing leadership behaviours, and gaining visibility within your organization will strengthen your candidacy and help you stand out, even against candidates who already have direct experience.

Also keep an eye out for 'learning assignments' or developmental roles. Some organizations create these opportunities with reduced requirements to help identify and grow promising talent.

And one final piece of advice: avoid making yourself indispensable in your current role. If you're the only one who can do your job, not only will it be hard for you to take a vacation - you may also have become unpromotable. A good leader builds their team members up to ensure that others can step into your role and succeed, which frees you up to take on new challenges and advance in your career.

In Short...Be Prepared

Breaking into management isn't about waiting reactively for the perfect opportunity—it's about actively preparing for it. By building your capabilities, aligning with organizational goals, and showing leadership in your current role, you'll be ready when that opportunity comes your way.

ABOUT THE AUTHOR

Gary Wilde. P.Eng., PMP

Gary is Director of IT Solutions at the Regional Municipality of Peel in Canada. Peel Region is consistently recognized at the employee and program level for its commitment to innovation and excellence in all service areas. He is also an Excellence in Teaching award-winning instructor with the University of Toronto School of Continuing Studies. Sharing his rich, real-life project, program, and portfolio management experiences, combined with his passion for teaching, makes Gary a popular instructor.

In the private and public sectors, he led diverse project teams in the fields of engineering and construction, power generation, energy management, corporate strategic projects, innovation, and IT. Gary has extensive experience working on international projects, having spent many years living and working across North America, South America, Asia, Africa, and the Middle East. He is a Professional Engineer and a Project Management Professional.

Gary is passionate about leading teams that develop technology solutions that make a positive difference in people's lives. His strengths are in bringing people along on a journey, building and growing teams, and organizing and managing complex work, and he has long held the motto "dare something worthy." Outside of work, you will find him researching the deep truths about the big questions in life.

When to Just Say "*Yes*"

Paula Wagner

I settled into a chair. Behind me, a picture of a cityscape glowed—a buzzing metropolis frozen in time. Lights flanked the camera, bathing the scene in an almost surreal clarity. Somewhere in the shadows, the interviewer's voice emerged, smooth but with a hint of mischief. "Is it okay if I ask you one more question?"

The dreaded wildcard question. I thrive on preparation, the kind of person who enjoys dissecting a problem until there's nothing left to chance. But sometimes, life calls for improvisation. I decided to take the leap. "Sure," I replied

The interviewer glanced at her notebook, brushing a stray strand of hair from her eyes. "If you had to give advice to someone early in their career, what would it be?"

I didn't hesitate. "Just say *yes*."

The words landed with more weight than I expected, even to me. They weren't rehearsed, they weren't part of my polished talking points. But as soon as they left my mouth, I knew they were right.

Of course, I elaborated, because "just say *yes*" in isolation can sound like an invitation to chaos. It's not about agreeing to everything without thought; it's about understanding that preparation is valuable, but opportunity rarely arrives with a perfect, neatly tied bow. In my career, saying *yes* has never been about blind optimism—it's been about recognizing when a challenge is worth the stretch. It's about leaning into growth, even when it's uncomfortable.

Looking back, the most pivotal moments in my career weren't the neatly scheduled milestones I had planned for. They were the moments when I said *yes* to something that made my pulse quicken. *Yes* to taking on a project that seemed beyond my expertise. *Yes* to stepping into a leadership role that required me to grow faster than I thought possible. *Yes* to conversations that weren't just transactional, but transformative—building networks, trust, and shared vision.

Saying *yes* became the foundation of my career, not because it's easy, but because it challenges you to adapt, grow, and discover capabilities you never knew you had. It's not about being reckless; it's about having the courage to embrace uncertainty and the confidence to trust that you'll navigate whatever comes your way.

That one word—*yes*—has opened doors I didn't even know existed. It's brought me to the forefront of innovation, challenged my leadership in unexpected ways, and reshaped how I think about opportunity. If there's one thing I've learned, it's that readiness isn't about having all the answers. Readiness is about having the confidence to step forward, knowing you'll learn as you go.

As the interview wrapped up, I found myself reflecting on how often we complicate career advice, turning it into a puzzle of strategies and formulas. The truth is the most powerful lessons are often the simplest. For me, saying *yes* wasn't just a piece of advice, it became a mindset, a philosophy that shaped every opportunity, every challenge, and every leap into the unknown.

If I could share one takeaway with anyone starting out, it would be this: Don't wait for perfection. Don't let fear convince you to sit still. Growth doesn't live in what you already know. It thrives in the unknown, in the *yes* that stretches you, challenges you, and reminds you that you're far more capable than you realize.

Say Yes to Bold Moves: The Power of Yes

Saying *yes* isn't about being a people-pleaser or a yes-person; it's about recognizing when a challenge holds the power to transform you. Early in my career, I was handed what could only be described as a classic hot mess. A project in utter disarray with no clear goals, no roadmap, and absolutely no volunteers. It was the kind of assignment that made most people suddenly fascinated by the floor tiles during team meetings.

My first instinct? Steer clear of it entirely. Wouldn't it be safer to stick to what I knew, where I was comfortable, where the risks were low? But I've learned that growth doesn't come from low stakes or well-trodden paths. Growth thrives in the spaces that scare us a little. So, I said *yes*.

Walking into that chaos felt like being dropped onto the set of an action movie without a script. I had no idea who the main characters were, let alone what roles they played. Back then, I didn't know to call them "key stakeholders" or "influencers." What I did know was how to work hard, and luckily for me, I had the time and energy to throw myself into the deep end.

I asked every question I could think of, even those that made me cringe the moment they left my mouth. 'What would you do in my shoes?' became my go-to icebreaker. Those candid conversations were treasure troves, not just for practical advice, but for deeper insights. Truly listening, not just hearing, allowed me to pick up on the subtleties: the pauses, the tone, and the unspoken truths that often revealed far more than the words themselves.

Through countless late nights, relentless effort, and guiding a team that often struggled to hit the same note, clarity appeared. Piece by piece, the project began to take shape. By the end, we delivered real results, results that mattered, and, more importantly, I walked away with a level of confidence I hadn't realized I lacked.

Some might think saying *yes* to a situation like that is impulsive or even reckless. But saying *yes* is not about throwing caution to the wind. It's about taking strategic risks, betting on yourself and your ability to adapt, learn, and deliver. If you never step outside the confines of what's comfortable, you'll never discover just how far you can stretch. And let's be honest: extraordinary outcomes rarely happen in the cozy corner of the status quo.

Over time, I've realized there are two types of *yes*: the *BIG yes* and the *little yes*.

The *BIG yes* is a game-changer. It's the decision that shifts your entire trajectory, a promotion, a career pivot, or stepping into a role that seems intimidatingly beyond your current capabilities.

The *little yes* is the unsung hero. It's the *yes* that builds momentum, taking on an unfamiliar task, volunteering for a small project, or lending your expertise to someone outside your department.

The magic lies in how these yeses build upon each other. The *BIG yes* sets the course; the *little yes* keeps the wheels turning. Together, they create a ripple effect of growth, a compounding of opportunities that can lead you places you didn't even know existed.

Saying *yes* to bold moves isn't just a career strategy, it's a life philosophy. It's about understanding that the most rewarding paths are rarely the easiest. Growth, opportunity, and success? They live just beyond the boundaries of certainty, waiting for the moment you're bold enough to say yes.

Say Yes to Curiosity: How Learning Paves the Way

When I was 16, I landed my first after-school job at an automobile dealership. Glamorous? Not exactly. My duties were the kind of mind-numbing tasks that made alphabetizing paperwork feel like a thrill ride. Every day, I passed by a framed cross-stitch hanging on a dark, wood-paneled wall, a relic of someone's attempt to inspire the uninspired. It read:

"Luck is when opportunity meets preparation."

At 16, I couldn't roll my eyes hard enough. Who has time to prepare for something that might never happen? I didn't understand it then, but that phrase planted itself in my brain, waiting for the right moment to bloom.

Fast forward to my 20s, and I finally started to get it. By then, I knew an MBA was going to be my ticket to the roles I wanted. So, I decided to go for it. But this wasn't your typical "career woman pursues degree" story. I turned it into a high stakes balancing act: full-time job? Check. Night classes? Check. A husband and a newborn baby thrown into the mix? Naturally.

Work-life balance? Let's just say the phrase was more of a theoretical concept during that phase of my life. Instead, I discovered something more valuable: perseverance. I learned that balance isn't about creating a perfect day where everything fits neatly into place. It's about seasons. Some seasons are for grinding—late nights, early mornings, and saying *no* to anything that doesn't align with your goal. Other seasons are for rest, reflection, and recalibrating.

It took me only five years to complete a two-year MBA program (yes, I see the irony). But every late-night study session, every sacrifice, and every exhausting drive home from class laid a foundation I couldn't have imagined. The degree wasn't just a line on my résumé, it became a springboard. It opened doors to opportunities I hadn't even considered. I became a visiting professor, co-authored a book with a professor I deeply admired, and most importantly, I was prepared when senior leadership roles came calling.

When opportunity knocked, I didn't just answer—I swung the door wide open, fully equipped and ready to own the moment.

But here's the twist: preparation wasn't just about the degree or the titles. The real game-changer was curiosity.

Curiosity transforms you from someone who follows instructions into someone who creates strategies. Every challenge I've faced has started with a simple but powerful act: asking questions. Why are we doing this? What's the ultimate goal? What could go wrong? How will we measure success? These questions aren't just about checking boxes, they're about peeling back layers, cutting through assumptions, and discovering insights others might have missed. Curiosity is more than a tool, it's a mindset, one that elevates every decision, every project, and every outcome.

Looking back, that cross-stitch wasn't just office décor. It was a career lesson disguised as needlework. Preparation isn't about trying to predict the future. It's about equipping yourself to handle whatever comes your way. And luck? It's not some roll of the dice. It's the reward for being ready when the right opportunity presents itself.

So, here's my advice: Say *yes* to learning. Whether it's enrolling in a degree program, volunteering for a stretch project, or simply asking better, sharper questions, every bit of preparation and curiosity adds up. One day, when the right door opens, you won't hesitate.

You'll stride through it, not as someone who got lucky, but as someone who created their own luck and seized their moment with confidence and purpose.

Final Thoughts: Just Say Yes

Saying *yes* isn't about diving headfirst into chaos without a plan, it is about stepping into the unknown with courage, curiosity, and a dash of wit. Sure, it might feel terrifying, like you're leaping off a cliff without fully knowing what's below. But here's the truth: saying *yes* is the secret ingredient that transforms a good career into a great adventure.

Along the way, you'll say *yes* to curiosity, and suddenly, you're not just ticking boxes, you're asking the questions that open doors and shape strategies. You'll say *yes* to resilience, tripping over obstacles and bouncing back with more strength (and maybe a good story to tell).

You'll say *yes* to building connections, not just collecting business cards, but forging relationships that help you grow and, sometimes, pull you through.

You'll learn to say *yes* to celebrating success, no matter how small, because every win is fuel for the next challenge. And most importantly, you'll say *yes* to creating your own opportunities, stepping up even when no one's asking, and proving to yourself and others what you're truly capable of.

Saying *yes* isn't about perfection, it's about progress. It's about turning setbacks into stepping stones, finding joy in the messy middle, and realizing that sometimes the best opportunities come disguised as challenges (or chaos). It's about showing up authentically, making others feel valued, and having the audacity to leap, knowing you'll figure out the landing.

The next time opportunity knocks or quietly taps while you're busy juggling a hundred things, don't hesitate. Open the door. Say *yes*. Dive in with the confidence that you'll figure it out, adapt, and grow along the way. Because in the end, it's not just about the destination; it's about the stories you gather, the lessons you learn, and the connections you build that make the journey unforgettable.

ABOUT THE AUTHOR

Paula Wagner

Paula Wagner is a trailblazing CIO and transformative technology leader who has redefined the impact IT can have on enterprise growth. She is known for building AI-native, future-forward organizations that don't just adapt to change—they anticipate it, lead it, and scale because of it. With a career spanning energy, media, hospitality, and insurance, Paula brings a powerful mix of technical depth, business savvy, and bold, outcome-driven leadership.

As Chief Information Officer at Mansfield Energy, Paula is architecting a sweeping transformation—turning a legacy business into a modern technology enterprise. She's elevated IT from support function to strategic powerhouse: embedding intelligence into operations, launching enterprise-grade digital platforms, and leading product teams deliver at a pace once thought impossible. Under her leadership, IT has become a core value creator—not just internally, but for Mansfield's partners and customers alike.

What drives Paula is the belief that technology, when done right, can fundamentally reshape how businesses operate and how people work. She is passionate about building high-performance cultures, mentoring future leaders, and leading organizations through inflection points with purpose and precision.

Her edge lies in her ability to turn ambiguity into direction—and direction into momentum. She sees around corners, galvanized teams, and executes with clarity and conviction. Whether she's reimagining legacy systems or unlocking new commercial opportunities with AI, Paula doesn't just keep pace—she sets it.

Because for Paula Wagner, the future isn't something you wait for—it's something you create.

When I Realized OCM Wasn't Enough: The Tactic That Changed Everything

Kevin Kracher

ERP Deployments: Why So Many Still Fail

ERP (Enterprise Resource Planning) deployments are notoriously risky. A quick online search turns up no shortage of horror stories—projects that went off the rails, disrupted operations, hit revenue hard, and left corporate reputations bruised. One of the most well-known examples is Hershey's infamous ERP failure in 1999, when system issues led to delayed Halloween shipments and significant financial losses.

What's surprising is how little has changed since then. Even today, companies across industries still suffer major setbacks tied to failed ERP implementations—operational slowdowns, budget overruns, and missed business objectives.

Entire consulting firms and countless books have been devoted to improving ERP outcomes. And yet, true success remains elusive.

So why do so many ERP programs struggle?

After managing more than 15 large-scale ERP initiatives in a variety of leadership roles, I've come to believe that while the science and methodology of ERP implementation matter, they aren't enough. There's an *art* to success—something more nuanced and human-centered that often gets overlooked.

Why Traditional OCM Isn't Enough

Talk to any ERP implementation expert, and you'll likely hear the usual list of success factors:

- Executive sponsorship
- Well-defined scope
- Robust deployment and cutover plans
- Process harmonization
- Clean, consistent data
- A solid data migration strategy
- Engaged business users

Everyone agrees that Organizational Change Management (OCM) is critical to ERP success. After all, ERP isn't just a technology project—it's a people project.

Most traditional OCM strategies focus on several well-established areas:

- Stakeholder engagement and communication
- Change impact assessments
- Training and knowledge transfer
- End-user engagement and support
- Leadership alignment and sponsorship
- Resistance management and cultural alignment
- Performance measurement and continuous improvement

These are all essential components. And yet, despite all this structure and intention, ERP deployments still often fall short.

Why? Because traditional OCM often misses one crucial layer of the organization: middle management.

The Middle Manager Blind Spot

One of the most common failure points in ERP deployments is the disconnect between trained end users and their direct supervisors. Traditional OCM efforts tend to focus heavily on executive sponsors and end users—often leaving out the crucial middle layer: managers and supervisors.

Here's what typically happens:

- Managers expect the same reports, workflows, and outputs as before.
- They assume their teams will perform at pre-deployment levels—immediately.
- They aren't aware of new compliance requirements, like segregation of duties.

This disconnect creates a frustrating environment for employees. They've been trained to follow new processes, but their managers still expect them to operate under the old rules.

You'll hear things like, *"I need the XYZ report I've always used,"* or see genuine surprise when a manager learns that one person can no longer both create and approve purchase requisitions.

Most managers don't anticipate the productivity dip that naturally follows ERP go-live. Instead, they push for the same level of performance without realizing their teams are still learning a new system and adjusting to different ways of working.

As I have often observed: "Change doesn't fail because people resist; it fails because managers expect the old system in the new world."

The "Push" Problem of Traditional OCM

I saw this issue up close during a major transformation program at the world's largest medical device and pharmaceutical manufacturer.

In the first phase of the program, I led the technical workstream while a colleague managed business readiness and OCM. The project had all the right ingredients: a healthy budget, a top-tier integration partner, and a dedicated OCM team. But despite those advantages, the organization still struggled post go-live—with drops in efficiency, widespread confusion, and overall dissatisfaction.

What went wrong?

The OCM strategy was heavily "push"-oriented, focused on broadcasting information outward, rather than engaging people where they were.

The integration partner followed a textbook industry approach:

- Enlist subject matter experts (SMEs) as trainers and change champions
- Push out communications and training from the project team
- Provide detailed documentation and process guides

The assumption was simple: if the project team created enough content, adoption would follow.

It didn't.

The OCM Myths That Undermine Adoption

That push-heavy strategy is built on three flawed assumptions—myths that continue to undermine successful adoption in ERP programs.

Myth 1: Executives Will Cascade the Change

Executives are usually well-versed in the project's business case, but they often lack visibility into how the change affects daily operations. As a result, they can't effectively communicate what they don't fully understand.

Myth 2: SMEs Are Natural Change Champions

Subject Matter Experts are typically selected based on availability—not influence or leadership skills. They're often overwhelmed, juggling documentation, system testing, peer training, and their regular job duties. They may be knowledgeable, but that doesn't automatically make them effective change agents.

Myth 3: Classroom Training Is Enough

Classroom training can transfer information, but it rarely drives lasting behavior change. Without operational context, managerial reinforcement, and real-world support, even the best training won't fully prepare employees for new systems and workflows.

A Different Approach: The POV Model

By the time we reached the second phase of the program—a large SAP Order to Cash deployment for the company's neurovascular division—I was asked to take on overall leadership across both technology and business readiness, including OCM.

Having learned from the challenges in phase one, I knew we needed a different approach. So I asked the OCM team to help me develop what I called the Point of View (POV) Model.

The POV Model: Leading Change Through the Manager's Lens

The Point of View (POV) Model is grounded in a simple but powerful idea:

Change management should be shaped by the perspective of managers and supervisors—not just the project team.

How the POV Model Works

The POV Model flips the traditional OCM approach. Instead of pushing information out from the project team, we focused on what *managers* needed to lead their teams through change.

We developed department-specific deliverables tailored to middle managers, including:

- System tests completed to date
- Key process changes and associated risks
- Role and responsibility impacts
- Changes to reporting structures and key reports
- Shifts in workload across departments
- Training requirements and system access needs

But the real power of the POV Model came from *who* delivered the message. Instead of external consultants or project leads, the content was presented by the managers' own SMEs and power users—people they trusted, who could explain the changes in their language and context.

This approach opened the door to two-way communication. Managers had the space to ask questions, clarify expectations, and prepare their teams not just technically—but operationally and behaviorally as well.

A Real-World Case: Neurovascular ERP Deployment

For the Neurovascular Order to Cash ERP deployment, we built customized POV decks for each key department—Sales Operations, Finance, Accounts Receivable, Warehouse & Distribution, and others.

We then held targeted workshops where SMEs presented these materials directly to department leaders and their teams.

Each deck included detailed, department-specific information. For example, the Sales Operations deck outlined key customer-facing impacts. One major change involved packing slips: previously, a single consolidated slip was used for all orders in a shipment. Under the new system, each order would generate its own individual pack slip. The team also flagged master data changes, including a new customer numbering scheme and how those numbers would now be generated.

These POV sessions were paired with robust Day in the Life (DIL) testing scenarios.

The results spoke for themselves:

- Users and leaders were fully aligned on expectations
- Common ERP adoption pitfalls were addressed in advance
- The transition caused zero customer disruption
- Executive leadership called the deployment *"flawless"*

Enhanced Engagement and Transparency

One of the most powerful outcomes of the POV approach was the level of engagement it generated across the organization. By shifting the change conversation down to the operational level, we created space for real dialogue, transparency, and shared ownership.

Suddenly, the ERP project wasn't something being *done to* employees—it was something they were *part of.* In peer-to-peer workshops led by trusted colleagues, employees had the chance to openly discuss what was changing, ask questions, and offer feedback on the training and support they were receiving.

These sessions gave employees a platform to comment on the quality of training materials, request more hands-on practice, and better understand how the changes would affect their specific roles. They also encouraged managers and team members to raise concerns, challenge assumptions, and shape how their departments prepared for go-live.

The result? A genuine sense of ownership. Employees felt seen, heard, and included—not sidelined. The process fostered trust and transparency—two essential ingredients for any successful technology transformation.

Key Takeaways

The success of any ERP deployment hinges not just on the right tools or training, but on the people who guide others through the change—especially those in the middle. Here's a summary of the most important lessons from the POV approach.

Insight	Why It Matters
ERP failures continue despite structured OCM	Traditional OCM overlooks middle managers
Middle managers shape day-to-day adoption	Their expectations drive team behavior
The "push" model misses operational context	Change can't be forced from the top down
SMEs and classroom training aren't enough	Behavioral change requires expectation alignment
The POV Model bridges the gap	It empowers managers with role-specific, actionable information

What Leaders Should Do Differently

To drive successful ERP adoption and long-term value:

1. **Engage Middle Managers Early**

   Give them the operational clarity and context they need to lead confidently.

2. **Challenge the Myths**

   Don't rely on executive trickle-down messaging, overloaded SMEs, or one-size-fits-all training.

3. **Use the POV Model**

Deliver targeted, department-specific content through trusted team members.

4. **Prepare for the Productivity Dip**

   Set realistic expectations for a temporary slowdowns, and support teams as they adjust.

By re-centering ERP change management around the people who lead day-to-day execution, organizations can move beyond checkbox OCM—and finally achieve the kind of adoption that sticks. Always remember, "The difference between change resistance and change readiness is the manager in the middle."

ABOUT THE AUTHOR

Kevin Kracher

Kevin Kracher is a globally experienced business technology leader who has driven enterprise-scale digital and ERP transformations for some of the world's most respected organizations. As the former Global Vice President of Information Technology for a Fortune 500 med-tech leader, he delivered high-impact initiatives across operations, supply chain, quality, and regulatory functions—consistently generating measurable improvements in performance, compliance, and cost efficiency.

With a leadership portfolio spanning more than 15 major ERP deployments, Kevin understands that successful transformation isn't just about technology—it's about people. He brings a practical understanding of why these initiatives often fail—not due to technical complexity, but because of overlooked human factors. His change leadership approach emphasizes middle management engagement, peer-to-peer communication, and operational transparency as critical levers for success.

A champion of people-first transformation, Kevin has built and led award-winning IT teams recognized for seven consecutive years as one of *Computerworld's* "Best Places to Work in IT." Known for his collaborative leadership style and global mindset, he has consistently achieved top-tier employee engagement scores while fostering cultures of trust, accountability, and innovation.

Today, Kevin advises companies as a fractional CIO and strategic consultant, helping organizations improve transformation outcomes, avoid common pitfalls, and unlock lasting value from their technology investments.

He lives with his wife in Northeastern Florida, where they enjoy the beach, fishing, and spending time with family.

When Leadership Begins: Creating a Path to Success

Monique Rivera-Hart

Becoming a leader can be an exhilarating experience. However, for those not groomed for leadership from the beginning, the transition can be stressful. And without the right focus or support, one may find the experience a turn-off and decide they don't want to try it again. Hence, preparation is an absolute must, and this outline will focus on the lessons I have learned in the hopes of helping you along your journey toward leadership.

The dictionary defines a leader as a person who commands a group, organization, or country. A recent Google AI response stated that, "A leader is someone who inspires, guides, and motivates others to achieve a common goal, often by taking initiative, making decisions, and ensuring their team has the support needed to succeed." All statements I agree with. However, how does a newly promoted individual become a good or even a strong leader when they've been working alongside their teammates as a peer and are not expected to be the boss? And how do they go about developing new teams, roles, and something new when everyone isn't on board? And finally, how does one convince their team to trust them and stay motivated during that journey?

Before we get started, I think it's only fair to share that although I'm passionate about what I do today, I never set out to be in cyber security, let alone build a program or lead multiple teams in this space. The truth is that roles like these just didn't exist when it was time for me to start thinking about a career. And the thought of a woman leading them just wasn't fathomable back then. When I entered the workforce, women were still being asked to resign when they got married or decided to have children. In fact, one company asked me to decline an offer in another department after I disclosed that I was pregnant. So, I think it's fair to say that I didn't take the conventional route and instead came up with my own path that led me to where I am today. Thankfully, my Type A/B personality (which includes a fondness for solving puzzles, the ability to remain calm through stressful situations, and my willingness to take ownership during challenging times or with difficult tasks) allowed others to take a chance on helping me become a leader.

My first leadership experience consisted of my boss delegating to me the role of Team Lead and requiring me to be the first point of contact for all my peers. I was instructed to help create the team outline and educate and train all new team members. I was told that the intention was for me to prepare to be promoted to team Supervisor. But, I failed!

Like many new managers, I initially leaned on books, my academic background, and feedback from my leaders to guide me. I focused on building strong relationships with my peers, which helped foster trust. However, I struggled to consistently collaborate on strategic initiatives and didn't clearly establish myself as a leader within the team. I also lacked the experience to communicate upward effectively—specifically, how to connect our team's day-to-day work with the broader company mission. These gaps ultimately contributed to my not being promoted at that time.

I quickly learned that I needed to build a small group of confidants that I could trust and learn from. I connected with individuals who were willing to share their lessons learned and provide honest feedback on the areas in which I still needed to grow. And, when the time came, I didn't hesitate to take a course or even return to school to strengthen my communication skills and grow in leadership and relationship-building.

Where do you start?

Before taking a leadership role, consider taking a personality type indicator like a Myers-Briggs assessment. Learn what your strengths and weaknesses are. Seek out team members who can fill in the gaps and help balance out your strengths and weaknesses. Consider the following when developing your team:

- Create an interview team to help find new hires for your group.
- Focus on building a multiskilled (diverse) team by deliberately seeking those with different skillsets and experiences.
- Be careful not to hire only those who remind you of yourself.
- Welcome those who question everything and need to understand the why before following your requests.
- Identify which individuals and roles the positions will interact with—both directly and indirectly—and determine which teams will be impacted by their work. Then, invite leaders and staff from those areas to participate in the interview process.
- When seeking a leader for a team, avoid including any direct reports who are also candidates for the role in the interview process to prevent a conflict of interest.

Once your team members have been selected and have accepted the job, consider postponing announcing their arrival. Give them the opportunity to learn the environment (for a couple of months) before being forced to make decisions—this works for both leadership and non-leadership roles. Make certain all new hires complete your company's onboarding process. And if your organization offers leadership training, enroll these individuals—regardless of their prior experience. It gives them valuable insight into your organization's culture and helps them understand why things operate as they do before they begin recommending changes. Read *The Leadership Challenge* by Kouzes and Posner for more information on best practices.

Know Your Teams—Who's on First?

When someone asks me about my team, they are usually taken aback by my response of *Which one?* When I first became a leader, I concentrated on what my direct reports were doing and needed. And while that was not a bad thing, I found that many times we would hit a brick wall because I hadn't taken the time to *collaborate* with my first team and instead would *inform* them of what we were doing. Yes, you read that right…my FIRST team, which today, I will tell you that my first team is my peers.

Although we were working toward the same goals—and often assumed we were aligned because we sat in the same meetings and heard the same directives—I learned the importance of clear communication and collaborating with my peers to establish a shared strategy and timeline *before* assigning tasks to my second team (aka: direct reports). Sometimes, this meant I had to hold separate strategy meetings or one-on-one conversations with my peer team to make certain we were in alignment and supporting each other's missions without causing (unintentional) conflict. This approach helped our teams stay motivated and work collaboratively without unnecessary frustration. More importantly, it reinforced a sense of consistency and alignment among the leadership team. Further, it allowed us to be more transparent with our teams—sharing the information they needed to pivot quickly when circumstances changed, and driving stronger, more collaborative outcomes. I highly recommend reading *The Speed of Trust* by Stephen Covey with Rebecca Merrill, and *Deep Change* by Robert E. Quinn for more information on building trust and inspiring success.

Can we really do that?

Sometimes the tasks we are given can feel impossible, but there's always a way to get things done.

Looking back, I've learned a lot from my early missteps. With over 20 years of experience leading teams, I've built new programs from the ground up at five different organizations. While I now oversee large teams, I didn't start that way. In every case, I was initially assigned to lead a team of fewer than five people—tasked with supporting several thousand. On paper, it looked like an impossible mission.

But I quickly discovered that success didn't depend on the size of the team—it came from focusing on the essentials first, rather than immediately trying to expand the department.

In each case, I asked the team to help identify what we needed to accomplish to support the organization's goals. I made it a point to include them in creating the prioritization plan and determining what was truly manageable with the staff we had. Together, we assessed not only what needed to be done, but who was best positioned to do the work.

This process helped us define the roles necessary to meet the mission—and allowed the team to grow organically, based on actual system needs. In some cases, that meant creating entirely new departments and roles that hadn't been part of the original plan.

More importantly, it allowed us to clearly outline our annual goals, track accomplishments, stay agile as technology evolved, create new opportunities for growth, and—crucially—celebrate the team's wins along the way.

Lessons learned and final thoughts

In summary, I've learned that my most effective tools as a leader are:

- listening, building trust through follow-through,
- collaborating and communicating consistently,
- being as transparent as possible, and sharing your intentions often, and
- celebrating your department's successes.

And remember, never miss an opportunity to communicate your wins and the value your team brings to leadership!

Lastly, invite your teams to be part of building the department's future. When people have a hand in shaping the work, they take ownership of its success.

For deeper insight on overcoming team challenges, I highly recommend *The Five Dysfunctions of a Team* by Patrick Lencioni.

Good luck on your journey—and as my mother always likes to say, *"If at first you don't succeed, try and try again, because nothing beats a failure but a try!"*

ABOUT THE AUTHOR

Monique Rivera-Hart

Monique Rivera-Hart is an award-winning, performance-driven leader with a strong track record of building, leading, and empowering high-performing teams across Cyber Security, Vulnerability Management, Incident Response, and Governance, Risk, & Compliance.

Recognized for developing and executing strategic initiatives that drive alignment between cybersecurity operations and overarching business goals across diverse industries including Healthcare, Bio-Medical, Food & Beverage, Media & Entertainment, Human Resources, Telecommunications, and Transportation.

When Yes is More

Todd Ryan

I got my first authentic taste of leadership as a practice in the early 1990s, during the first few years of my Information Technology (IT) career. I worked for Electronic Data Systems (EDS), a company fully immersed in the Franklin Covey approach to personal and organizational effectiveness. Every employee received a Franklin Planner, and we had to attend classes on how to use it to align our time with EDS's mission and values. I was hooked.

Over the years, I continued my studies individually and through corporate campaigns. By the time I was in the second decade of my IT career, I considered myself a book expert in leadership. If you moved my cheese, I knew exactly how to find it. Starting with a simple "Why," with just 7 habits and 21 irrefutable laws, I could leap from good to great, winning friends and influencing people, and still make time to eat (last, of course).

I've even witnessed a few well-meaning attempts to put the concepts from leadership books and seminars into practice. At various employers, I was invited to join corporate initiatives billed as "paradigm shifts"—usually branded with a catchy name (bonus points if it formed an acronym), handed out with some company swag, and launched at an off-site afternoon retreat led by a professional facilitator and attended by a very enthusiastic executive team. Unfortunately, the gravitational pull of the cultural status quo was strong, and the changes rarely lasted longer than the lettering on the t-shirts and frisbees.

As a manager, I tried to put many of the principles I had read about into practice but quickly became aware that my results were tempered by three critical factors: company policies, executive leadership, and the behavior of other managers. With varying levels of success, typically, the best I could achieve was to create a shield for my team. If your staff or other employees often told you, "I was actively looking for another job before you came along," "Thank you for protecting us," or "I don't ever want your job," you've probably experienced those challenges.

My observations baffled me as I knew I wasn't the only person who read these books during my career journey. I also learned the background of some of the leaders I met and was confident they had experienced the effects of effective executive leadership at various levels of the organization. So, where was the disconnect?

Later in my career, I had the great fortune of a front-row seat at an organization where I saw practical leadership principles come to life. It was exhilarating to witness those principles in action—from the executive suite to the front lines—and deeply gratifying to realize that they work! I watched as a prominent organization underwent a profound transformation in its mission, vision, and values. I've never been prouder to be part of a team.

For the first time in my career, I never wondered what the CEO would want me to do or what decision to make. Our leadership team was fully aligned with our mission, vision, and values, and I made decisions and spoke on behalf of the CEO with complete confidence. I didn't need to ask—I already knew. I understood why I was there and what we stood for.

Even more importantly, I finally understood the often overlooked disconnect between leadership theory and real-world business. Your drive, skills, and ambition might get you into a leadership seat, but your character makes you effective once you're there. There's no shortage of tips and tricks for climbing the ladder, but far less wisdom on navigating the dangers that can follow success. Maintaining influence and integrity after achieving authority takes just as much focus, discipline, and humility as it took to get there in the first place.

We've all seen what it looks like when someone achieves success and turns their focus inward. Virtually overnight, that employee moves from "one of us" to "one of them." Once there, they tell themselves that this is all due to *their* hard work and embrace the power and perks they believe they have earned and deserve.

As a result, they become disconnected from the people they are responsible for leading. They tell subordinates that returning to the office is not a big deal as they grab the keys to their company car. They show pictures of their vacation home at the all-hands meeting while their employees struggle to find an affordable one-bedroom apartment within commuting distance. Explain the reasoning behind their decisions that conflict with published company values? Pfft. The worker bees would never understand.

Even worse, they grow protective of their position and skilled at recognizing influential leaders in their organization and mentoring them while strategically limiting their potential.

But inward focus rarely satisfies, and what was at first unimaginable riches quickly becomes inadequate. We're all vulnerable to that temptation; most remember when we would wistfully think, "If only I made x dollars per year, I would be happy," or "If I could be a *Senior* Widget Maker." Those types of goals, once achieved, are quickly replaced with a new desire. The endless pursuit of "more" can be a great motivator, but it must be kept in perspective. If not, that line of thinking can quickly turn toxic as a leader and even lead us to sabotage our leadership position.

So, how do we *continue* to be leaders once we *are* leaders?

For the balance of this chapter, I'll share the principles used by ineffective leaders that I believe were their biggest downfalls. With each example, I will share how I saw great leaders guard against these downfalls, and I'll also share suggestions to protect against them. These principles differentiate between those in positional leadership, seemingly for their benefit, and those who use their platform to leave a legacy.

We must maintain self-awareness

Problem: Before stepping into leadership, you likely learned to stay vigilant—carefully managing your image, how you interacted with others, and how you were perceived. You understood the importance of being a thoughtful, effective communicator because your progress depended on it.

But that vigilance can fade once you reach the comforts of the C-suite. Feedback becomes scarcer at the top. No one is likely to raise their hand during an all-hands meeting to tell you that your words have alienated or disenfranchised people. The higher you rise, the less candid input you receive—especially about the things that matter most.

Protection: You must intentionally create a safe environment to receive meaningful feedback. That means building trust, offering psychological safety, and—where necessary—providing anonymity. Most importantly, you must *relentlessly pursue* feedback, especially when it's difficult to hear.

One powerful approach is to establish an employee improvement team that reflects your organization's diversity—particularly voices from underrepresented groups. Meet regularly with this team (or their elected representatives) and make it clear that their input is welcome and protected. Let them know that honest feedback will never result in retaliation. Encourage employees to connect with whichever team members they feel most comfortable speaking to, and use your position to model inclusivity and trust in every conversation.

Even simple actions—like ensuring everyone is heard—can influence how people engage with one another beyond those meetings. Trust takes time, but once it's there, honest feedback will follow.

It's also vital to seek feedback from beyond your organization or sphere of influence—people who aren't afraid to challenge you. For me, that came in the form of an Info~Tech counselor. She regularly irritated me in the best possible way. I needed her experience and objectivity to keep my ego in check. No one else spoke to me the way she did—poking, prodding, and pushing me into uncomfortable territory. And while I didn't always enjoy those conversations, I grew from every single one, both personally and professionally.

We must subdue our arrogance

Problem: Success tends to cause us to believe we are always right.

After all, being good at everything you do landed you in this seat, right? That thought, if left unchecked, can create blind spots that can grow to obscure your ability to accept any idea that isn't yours. When that happens, your entire organization is limited to the intelligence and creativity of one individual rather than harnessing the collective wisdom and creativity that diversity of thought brings. Don't confuse everyone agreeing with your ideas with a collaborative organization.

Protection: Use your influence to help others succeed, not to enforce your beliefs.

Bring your leaders problems to solve, not programs to implement. Allow them to express themselves creatively so you can fully leverage their experiences and insight. Your ideas should be a fail-safe when no other practical solutions are available. Even then, your ideas should serve merely as conversation starters.

Punish patterns, not mistakes. Allowing your staff to make mistakes will enable them to grow, innovate, and create. One of the most important lessons you can help them learn is managing their mistakes. Use their mistakes as an opportunity to teach them transparency, continuous improvement, communication, and logic, all of which will serve them well.

We must refocus our pride

Problem: Excessive pride leads us to false self-dependence.

Unlike arrogance, which insists you're always right, pride quietly inflates your sense of how much of your success is self-made. It tempts you to take full credit for the initiatives you led—while conveniently overlooking the contributions of those who did much of the work. Pride is the single raindrop that believes it caused the flood.

Protection: Use your platform to bestow power and authority upon others.

For example, at a meeting with a vendor or another department, introduce one of your developing staff members by saying, "I want to introduce Jane as she will be an important contact. Jane is quickly becoming our top expert in this initiative, and it would be wise for your organization to interact with her as much as possible." You've set Jane up for success in just two sentences and telegraphed your support.

Similarly, look for opportunities to empower tomorrow's leaders by identifying performance *and* motive—then providing opportunity. In what I believe is one of life›s greatest secrets, simply saying *yes* to someone else›s growth can play a part in their success and, in some cases, change the course of their life.

For me, it starts with spotting individuals who are already performing or clearly have potential and then taking the time to understand what drives them. I seek those with a motivation that transcends a 5% raise or a title bump. I look for underemployed individuals who pursue excellence not for recognition but because of their values.

To me, the hallmark of a great leader is someone who actively embraces those who want their job someday—and mentors them to be ready for it. They're not a threat. They're your legacy. The people you invest in will never forget your belief in them; chances are, they'll pay it forward.

In my experience, few things are more exhilarating or rewarding than living out this principle.

The impact of *yes*

My most meaningful career achievements haven't been promotions or awards. They've been the minor roles I played as a background character in someone else's inspirational story. Below are a few recent examples of how these principles can translate into a lasting leadership legacy.

I once interviewed a young woman for an entry-level role. When I asked what drives her, she fought back tears and shared that she was a first-generation U.S. citizen. Her parents had made sacrifices to give her this opportunity, and she felt a deep responsibility not to disappoint them. A few years later, she held one of the most senior technical roles in the organization, with top-tier certifications. One of the proudest moments of my life was when she asked me to write her recommendation letter for a doctoral program. She did all the work—I just said *yes.*

Another time, I met a curious and driven young man working a non-technical, repetitive job. I later hired him for an entry-level technical position. He had a passion for solving problems and helping others, and he absorbed every bit of technology we threw his way. He worked hard, rose to executive leadership, and even surpassed my career trajectory. He became a lifelong friend. All I had to do was say *yes.*

Later, a principled young man in a mid-level technical role asked me relentless questions about leadership—always wanting to understand the "why" behind every decision. As I got to know him, it became clear that he would never sacrifice his values for fame or fortune. When I left the organization, I campaigned for his promotion to a C-level role—a campaign that mostly involved convincing *him* he was ready. The organization agreed. Today, he continues to build on our shared vision and values, taking them further than I ever could have. He still credits me for part of his success, even though all I did was say *yes.*

Looking back on my career—the people I met and the times I was fortunate enough to say *yes*—it's clear that our true legacy is people, not personal fame or fortune. I only became a C-level executive because someone said *yes* to me. (Technically, she told me to stop saying *no* when she told me she was promoting me. Oftentimes, leadership means convincing others they're capable.)

I could fill this book with stories of the people who said *yes* to me and those I had the privilege of supporting in return. Yes, success often comes with financial rewards—but when you consider the generational impact of helping someone change their career trajectory, the value transcends words.

So, pursue your goals. Harness your ambition. Achieve whatever success you desire. But don't lose sight of the people around you along the way. Be self-aware. Be humble. And whenever you can—say *yes.*

ABOUT THE AUTHOR

Todd Ryan

Todd Ryan is a Senior Director with a global learning management corporation. With over three decades of experience, Todd has earned a reputation as a highly adaptable technical expert and a charismatic leader with a high level of emotional intelligence that he leverages to bring out the best in others.

Previously, Todd spent well over a decade as CIO and CTO, leading information technology departments for large local governments. Todd understood the power of working cooperatively with others, especially in cybersecurity maturity. He used his influence to build connections and allies across the state and nation to raise the collective local government cybersecurity footprint. Todd successfully led his organizations through multiple national security level one events and was frequently consulted at the local, state, and national levels for his efforts to develop cybersecurity leadership for the common good.

Todd is passionate about championing those at a disadvantage or underrepresented and is drawn to mission-oriented organizations. With a strong preference for action over words, Todd uses his platform as a leader to lift and further the career of others. Few things motivate Todd more than being told something can't be done and allowed to try. Some of his greatest joy came from seeing the impossible become reality, especially when he was able to help others achieve greatness.

A lifelong introvert in deep undercover as an extrovert, you'll find Todd recharging his batteries, enjoying quiet contemplation, and experiencing the natural wonders of Atlanta, GA, and surrounding areas with his family and friends.

When You Trust Change to Lead You Forward

Marline Thomas

We all have a story to tell. Looking back, it's the significant events that shape who we become. But we don't stop there—we keep evolving. And that, I've learned, is the secret to longevity in this business.

I was born in a small town in the southwest of Puerto Rico. My childhood was difficult in many ways. I always seemed to be getting into trouble, but the one saving grace was that I was very smart. But being smart was a double-edged sword. Good grades helped me get out of trouble, but I didn't want to be labeled a nerd or a geek, so I kept acting out.

Just as I was starting high school, I learned about the Residential Center of Educational Opportunities of Mayagüez, C.R.O.E.M., a prestigious science and math-focused school that only accepts a select few students each year. To get in, you needed a GPA above 3.5, strong letters of recommendation, a good score on a standardized test, and a successful interview.

But it wasn't the prestige that drew me in; it was the chance to finish high school a year early. Many people doubted I could do it, which only made me more determined to prove them wrong. I made the cut, and I graduated early. Goal achieved.

I was accepted into the University of Puerto Rico with full academic and Army ROTC scholarships, my first step on the path to becoming a doctor, or so I thought. I had just turned 17 the month after I started college, and the truth is, I wasn't mentally, emotionally, or socially prepared for that new environment. On top of that, I didn't have solid study habits. In high school, I could glance at a book for a few minutes and still ace the test. But that approach didn't cut it in college. Over the next two years, a lot happened, and eventually, I lost my scholarship.

But I wasn't about to return home a failure. So, I made a bold choice: I enlisted in the U.S. Army.

I took the aptitude test, and every job they offered me was in technology. I couldn't picture myself as a technician. Technology felt completely foreign. When I thought of it, I imagined NASA scientists with thick glasses and pocket protectors. There were no personal computers, no cell phones, none of the advanced electronics that are everywhere today.

The recruiter kept insisting that technology was the way of the future. He told me people would kill for the kinds of opportunities I had. Eventually, I picked one of the options they gave me and headed off to learn about circuits, resistors, capacitors, electronic schematics, precision soldering, programming, networking and more.

But before I could dive into technology, I had to survive Basic Training at Fort McClellan, Alabama. That alone was a major culture shock. The Army helped me channel my energy and opened a door into a field I never would've chosen on my own. This was the first turning point in my evolution.

Throughout most of my military career, I was often the only woman in the room. As a Hispanic female in a male-dominated environment, I had to hold my own or be eaten alive. There was no space to push for major changes in the culture around me. It was an excruciating journey, but also incredibly rewarding.

I spent over a decade on active duty. I married another soldier, and together we had three sons. Being a dual-military family brought its own set of challenges, and eventually, our marriage didn't survive. The deployment to Saudi Arabia during the first Gulf War and the one-year hardship tour in South Korea were especially difficult.

I was a single parent with three young boys, stationed at Fort Bragg, North Carolina, when I received orders for another hardship tour—this time back to South Korea. That was the moment I knew it was time to leave the Army. I loved my military career and would've stayed the course, but my kids needed stability. The Army has many soldiers. My sons had only one mom.

Time to change again! This was a major transition because the military was all I had ever known. I joined a managed hosting company in Atlanta, Georgia. I left the military on a Friday and started my civilian job the very next Monday.

I advanced quickly, largely because I volunteered for challenges and consistently showed I could take on more responsibility and deliver results. I managed major data center migrations, supported companies across various industries, built teams, and slowly found my footing in the civilian world.

The company continued to grow and was eventually acquired. Then, my position was eliminated, and for the first time in my adult life, I found myself without a job.

Sometimes we choose change, and other times circumstances beyond our control force it upon us. My GI Bill was about to expire, so I worked as a contractor while pursuing my Master of Business and Technology at the University of Georgia. During that time, I gained experience with global organizations in two more industries: hospitality and healthcare. I also discovered that contracting is not for me.

With every engagement, I added more tools to my toolbelt. I learned about SOX compliance and how to manage customers across different industries while working with a managed hosting company. It was fascinating to see how manufacturing and retail approached the end-of-year holiday season. The manufacturing companies we supported shut down their plants for the last two weeks of the year, which gave us time to complete maintenance or implement changes without worrying about downtime. For retailers, however, this same period was absolutely critical. From Thanksgiving through the first week of January, there was a complete freeze. No changes could be made. At the hospitality company, I began working with global distributed teams and saw firsthand the challenges of coordinating maintenance windows across multiple countries and time zones.

Throughout my career, I've witnessed and adapted to major technological shifts, from SCO Unix to Windows, the World Wide Web, distributed computing, Wi-Fi, Y2K, USB, SD-WAN, AI, virtualization, IoT, and many more. I learned early on that specializing in just one area can lead to obsolescence. To stay relevant, I've made it a point to continuously evolve my skills. My journey began with reading schematics and replacing faulty components, and over time, my expertise has grown to include system administration, networking, programming, project management, service delivery, and operations management. In this field, adaptability isn't optional, it's essential.

On a personal level, I learned that the conflict resolution approach I used in the military did not translate well to the civilian world. Remember what I said about holding my own? I believed I couldn't show any weakness. I was always on guard, constantly looking for signs that someone might try to put me down. That posture served me well in the military, where it was a necessary defense mechanism. In the civilian sector, however, the environment required more finesse and nuance. My straightforward, no-nonsense attitude needed adjustment.

I had to develop emotional intelligence. Empathy, self-control, and both emotional and situational awareness became critical skills for personal and professional growth. There are many leadership models to draw from, including participative, charismatic, directive, authoritarian, servant, and paternalistic styles. My approach shifts depending on the situation, but at my core, I am motivated by a desire to serve, build community, and foster a sense of belonging. As a servant leader, I have the confidence to guide and the empathy to support. When people see your passion and commitment through your actions, they want to connect with you. Shared values and behaviors become the foundation for engagement, innovation, and high performance.

Throughout my life, I have faced my fair share of obstacles, each one serving as a catalyst for personal growth. I discovered that the key to staying relevant is a combination of continuous learning, evolution, and meaningful relationship building. Many people invest so heavily in their work identity that they struggle to define who they are outside of it. It's important to remember that you are much more than your profession.

Evolving doesn't mean becoming someone else. What matters most is staying true to your core values as you grow. Welcome change and the unknown, as they hold the key to self-discovery and a life enriched by new experiences. Embrace challenges. They have the power to shape you into the person you aspire to become.

"Set your course by the stars, not the lights of every passing ship."

- Omar N. Bradley

ABOUT THE AUTHOR

Marline Thomas

Marline Thomas is a Puerto Rico-born U.S. Army veteran and accomplished technology executive with a proven track record of leading complex digital transformations and building high-performing teams. Her career spans over two decades across both the public and private sectors, where she has combined strategic vision with hands-on technical expertise to drive innovation and operational excellence.

After proudly serving in the U.S. Army, Marline transitioned into the tech industry, where she quickly established herself as a leader known for her integrity, resilience, and results-driven leadership style. Her work has included enterprise IT modernization, infrastructure, service operations, and business process automation. She is also a passionate advocate for diversity in tech and mentors young professionals pursuing careers in STEM.

Marline's leadership is marked by her commitment to service, her deep understanding of technology's role in shaping the future, and her dedication to empowering the next generation of leaders.

When Times are A-Changin'

Robert Sheesley

The year was 1992. Six months had passed since my Operation Desert Storm deployment with the United State Marine Corps, and I was settling back into civilian life as a Systems Engineer at Electronic Data Systems (EDS). It was good to be home.

Two moments that year stood out: a friend's request for me to lead a county campaign office for Ross Perot's presidential run, and a leadership internship session with Peter Senge, author of *The Fifth Discipline*, on EDS's Plano, Texas campus. The irony wasn't lost on me—EDS was Ross's creation. That session, and multiple readings of Viktor Frankl's *Man's Search for Meaning* during my military deployment, shaped my perspective on change—how to understand, plan, and lead it. The timing was fitting. I had just been promoted to Systems Engineer Supervisor. However, volunteering at the age of 27 to lead a campaign office was an unexpected challenge, and an exciting opportunity. Freshly back at EDS, I found myself at the start of a lifelong journey in Organizational Change Management (OCM)—a journey that continues to this day.

Understanding the Psychology of Change

Psychology is the science of human behavior, especially in relation to awareness, emotion, and motivation. Change is transformation. Together, the psychology of change is the study of how people respond to transformation—an essential skill for leaders guiding organizations forward. Winning hearts and minds starts with engaging stakeholders, including employees, partners, customers, and investors.

Change leaders will benefit from an understanding of some of the predictable states people go through when confronting and processing change. People facing change often fall into one of two roles: victim or opportunist. Victims resist, saying, "This will never work" or "I have no voice here." Opportunists embrace the challenge. Wise leaders anticipate resistance and address it proactively, emphasizing the "WHY" behind change (as Simon Sinek shares in '*Start with Why:* How Great Leaders Inspire Everyone to Take Action"). Let's examine the predictable states people experience when confronting change.

Awareness – People first become aware of change through observation, announcements, or conversations. While they may grasp the basic intent, they often don't fully absorb the deeper *why*, leaving them without a true aha moment.

Resistance – Resistance is a natural reaction, both conscious and unconscious. Employees who don't see the benefits often perceive change as unfair, leading to fear and pushback—what's known as *resistance to change (RTC).*

Confusion – Early awareness rarely includes all the details, leading people to fill in the gaps themselves—often with fear-based assumptions. Messages like *"Improve productivity"* may be misinterpreted as *"Fewer jobs,"* while *"Best practices"* may be heard as *"More restrictions."*

Enthusiasm (or Skepticism) – People make judgments based primarily on how they believe the change affects them personally. Some see the change process as an opportunity to provide more significant input and influence; others see it as a management scheme to get more work out of them. The polarity of this state is typically influenced by the react versus respond choice.

Learning – The change process is a cycle of learning. People gradually (eventually) learn to understand the **WHY**, the whole system, and the implications on their job, their job security, their relationship(s) with others, and their job satisfaction.

Effort – Once the change process begins, people will typically focus on their work, understanding their jobs as part of a system, taking ownership of their role in the process(es), and extending effort to "make it work" or "find improvement."

Doubt – As learning and effort increases, doubts will arise. Some people will question the entire effort, saying it will not work, that it will not last, that it is not worth additional effort, and will argue that performance is worse, not better.

Acceptance – Observed results from an ongoing effort will produce some level of acceptance of the change. The **WHY** begins to receive acknowledgement of its validation. Acceptance of the new way manifests as benefits (e.g., time savings, cost savings, easier work, improved quality) are observed, measured and reported as outcomes of the change.

Belief – As results continue, and increase in magnitude (value) is realized, the effort of adoption and use becomes increasingly more comfortable. People will gain faith and trust in the change, and the change leader. New habits will form and people will develop a belief in and advocacy for the new system.

At 15 months into my career, I was notified that the U.S. was entering a military campaign in the Middle East, and my infantry battalion was activated for Operation Desert Storm. The events over the next year shaped my understanding of human response versus reaction, a theme Dr. Frankl explores in *Man's Search for Meaning* through his experiences in Auschwitz. My deployment and reflection on Frankl›s work helped me understand how people process change and its tangible and intangible impacts. This experience became a foundation for my approach to helping organizations navigate and implement change.

Dr. Frankl's key insight is that "Between stimulus and response there is a space. In that space is our power to choose our response. In our response lies our growth and our freedom." Recognizing this space and using it to guide responses is one of the most powerful tools for navigating change. For the change consumer, it's like waking up from The Matrix. For the change architect, it's about understanding how humans process change, and applying strategies to help organizations succeed.

The observation and recognition of leaders of change that this space exists and that one can make use of it to help stakeholders choose a response is one of the most impactful contributions on can make as a leader of change in pursuit of positive outcomes and the avoidance of negative experiences. For the stakeholder, its profundity is akin to having taken the red pill and being awoken from The Matrix. And all it took to get started was to be aware. For the change leader, it is first the cerebral understanding of the various ways humans process change and the application of methods, techniques, processes and communication that serves to create and facilitate the understanding that will determine the success of organizational change.

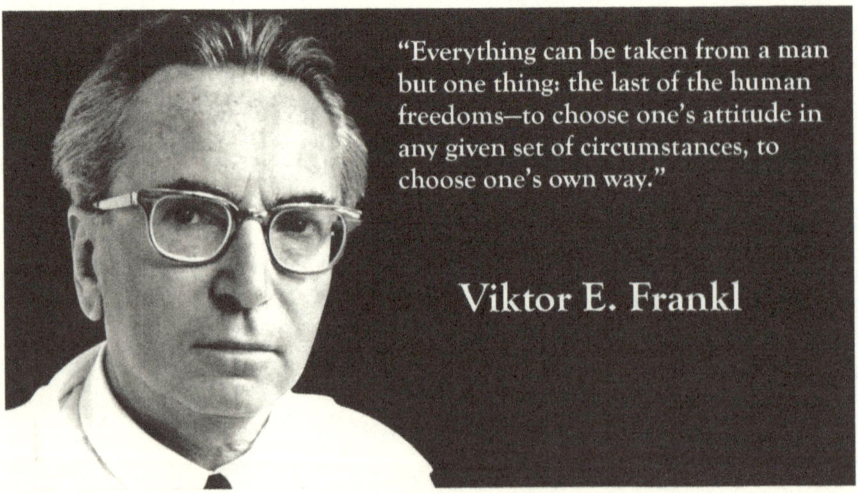

Reaction vs. Response

According to Psychology Today (2016), a reaction is instantaneous, driven by unconscious beliefs, biases, and prejudices. It happens in the moment, without considering long-term consequences. We've all experienced the regret of wishing we could take back a comment or unsent email. A reaction is survival-oriented, often serving as a defense mechanism.

In contrast, a response is usually slower and considers both the conscious and unconscious mind. It's more "ecological," taking into account the well-being of others and weighing long-term effects, remaining aligned with core values.

In *Man's Search for Meaning*, Dr. Frankl shares his experiences as a prisoner in Nazi concentration camps during the Holocaust, detailing the horrific and inhumane conditions he endured while highlighting the importance of finding "meaning in life" even amidst unimaginable suffering. His story and the reality of his writings relative to change and the ability to confront, overcome and survive the negative circumstances of change would require multiple chapters of analysis, reflection, examination and commentary. However, we can learn from his thoughtful perspective on the ability of the human mind to process and seek meaning in change, no matter how it is delivered. His reflections on the human mind's ability to process and find meaning in change are profound. Perhaps his most relevant insight for leading change is: "When we are no longer able to change a situation, we are challenged to change ourselves."

During Peter Senge's talk in the EDS auditorium, one key takeaway was that familiarity and comfort are the enemies of change. Think about it: what are we most familiar with? Routine, ourselves, family, home, electronics. When change is imposed on us, we naturally resist. Is it the threat to our comfort and familiarity?

Peter Senge's most famous quote is: "People don't resist change. They resist being changed." As leaders of change, it's our responsibility to address this resistance, ensuring that people respond in support of the change rather than oppose it. He challenged us to reflect on a difficult life change we've experienced and how it was tough to accept over time.

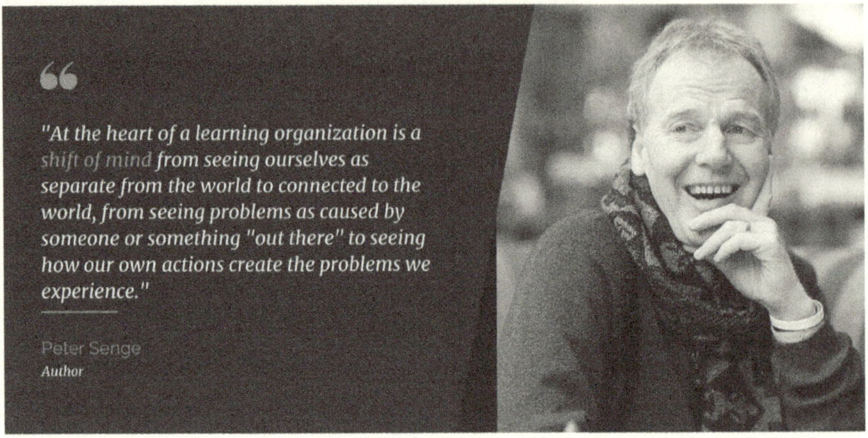

Fast forward to 1997, my first leadership role at Andersen Consulting after seven years at EDS, where I helped a healthcare client execute the largest health plan merger in history—two Blue Cross Blue Shield plans in three of the six largest U.S. cities. Our success in implementing this large-scale change was due to our focus on organizational change management, including forecasting synergies, creating business cases, and designing clear communications. By managing the changes in staggered phases over three years, we avoided overwhelming or underwhelming the teams.

In 2008, I led the merger integration of two large U.S.-based dental health plans. We helped our client select a new operating system and created a multi-year program with data, systems, and process workstreams. To win the hearts and minds of employees, we branded the effort as the "Business Transformation Program," emphasizing scope, timing, governance, and growth strategy. While we had the technology, governance, and processes, something was missing.

What about the people? How would we engage them to support and adopt the change? I met with the CEO and referenced a Harvard

Business Review study where 89% of CEOs cited a lack of investment in organizational change management (OCM) as the one thing they would change in large-scale implementations. That was the key insight. The CEO, a smart leader from Boston, approved the OCM resources to plan and manage the workstream, including stakeholder readiness assessments, communication strategies, and activities. Together, we designed a merger integration program with four primary workstreams, one of which was organizational change management. The completion of the merger consolidation was ultimately celebrated as a success.

Successful and winning organizations survive and thrive using a disciplined and culture-adaptive approach to program management and a responsive, flexible and effective organizational change management approach.

Barriers to Change

During Peter Senge's workshop, he shared a provocative thought: "The accumulation and use of positional authority is often threatened by change." Understanding whose authority might be threatened or supported by change is critical when planning and executing a change management strategy. Beyond positional authority, informal leaders—those with no official title but significant influence—are key to successful change. These individuals can gain grassroots support, address concerns, and facilitate change at the employee level.

Acknowledging potential obstacles allows change leaders to prepare effectively and plan for change-enabling activities, creating a change journey dashboard to track success, similar to that of a instrumentation panel found in the cockpit of an airplane that helps guide the journey to a successful landing. By beginning with the end in mind (thank you Stephen Covey) and defining success from the start—considering stakeholder response and engagement—the change team can reverse storyboard the journey, plan milestones, and make adjustments as necessary. A strong communication strategy focused on the "WHY" of change is crucial for overcoming these barriers. Developing communications and deploying resources to counter the obstacles referenced below will prove advantageous to the change leader and the success of the change.

Some common barriers to successful change include:

- **Uncommitted Leadership** Leaders must model the change and influence others to do the same.
- **Resistance to Change** Active and passive resistance must be identified and managed through proactive communication and tailored change plans.
- **Process Gaps** Organizations must update processes to meet best practices, avoiding pitfalls like "not invented here."
- **Adapting to New Roles and Responsibilities** Employees' skills must be aligned with evolving roles, demonstrating empathy and investment in their development. Adapting from the inside out is essential for successful change.

Additional Barriers to Change (as referenced by Senge):

- Individuals don't see the value of change.
- Team members don't "feel" empowered to change.
- Training fails to help participants understand how to behave differently.

- Rewards and evaluations are inconsistent with promoting the desired change.
- Leadership expectations don't align with the desired behavior change.
- A focus on short-term goals hinders long-term progress.
- Customers and suppliers are excluded from planning.
- Leadership has not taken on a sponsorship role.
- No action has been taken to bridge gaps in readiness for change.
- There is no two-way feedback channel to gauge sentiment.

Understanding these barriers allows change leaders and the OCM team to assess the organization—looking for signs that may foster these issues or recognizing if they've impacted previous change initiatives. Identifying these potential obstacles is critical to building an effective change strategy and plan. For each barrier, ask, "What can I do to overcome this?" This process informs your strategy, ensuring your plan is well-rounded. Failing to plan is planning to fail—so take the time to thoroughly prepare for leading and navigating the change journey.

Engaging in Robust Communications

A strong communications program—both internal and external—is essential for navigating change and should be established early in the planning stages. Employees and stakeholders expect leadership to be open and honest about the reasons for change, the new business processes, and what the change means for them. The "What's in it for me?" factor is critical: Will there be job changes, layoffs, plant closings, departmental shifts, or new responsibilities?

In large-scale change initiatives, such as mergers or acquisitions, employees will naturally feel anxious. A lack of communication creates a vacuum in which misinformation and rumors can spread, leading to mistrust and distractions that undermine the change process. This can result in lack of support and the departure of key employees.

To avoid this, it is crucial to communicate regularly, listen, and engage in Q&A sessions. Use clear language that shows leadership understands the employees' concerns. Take nothing for granted.

While communication strategies should be tailored to the organization, they should always emphasize disseminating information early and often. Communication may come from top executives via town halls or memos, or from business unit leaders through smaller meetings. A combination of methods may work best. Regardless of the approach, ensure the communication is consistent and synchronized with external messaging to business partners and customers.

The Impact of HUMALOGY®

Scott Klososky, founder and CEO of webcasts.com, an early producer of webcasted media ranging from corporate and government communications to sporting events and entertainment, founder of start-up Alkami Technology, a second-generation online banking platform and co-founder of Future Point of View, a technology-strategy consultancy, developed the concept of **HUMALOGY®**. **HUMALOGY®** is the science and art of blending of humans and technology. In essence it strives to define the optimal integration of humans and technology to complete work and produce value. Why does this matter?

In applying **HUMALOGY®** as a lens to evaluate business models, domains, and/or functions within an organization, we are able to target an optimal balance of how much human effort and how much technology is optimal to derive the greatest value possible. The **HUMALOGY®** scale is a ten-point metered range of concentration of technology and human effort in any given capability or process. This scale offers a visualization of the correct balance between technology and human effort. The correct balance will be different for each capability or process. For example, the optimal Human-to-Technology balance marketing to potential customers may be different than how you respond to current customer complaints and concerns.

As we plan for change, aligning any proposed change that requires some level of effort and acceptance with the strategy of the organization, the likelihood of success will be greater if the change leader and OCM team have a good understanding of where the functions, capabilities or processes are impacted by the change are on the **HUMALOGY®** scale. The more we can see the world (and our business) through the lens of **HUMALOGY®** the more we are able to assess and gauge the required acceptance and support needed by humans in the organization to implement the change for optimum results. The insights of a **HUMALOGY®** scale analysis will serve to inform the degree of impact as well as effort necessary to apply to the change strategy and plan, and specific areas of need. As a very recent example of the use of technology that might challenge conventional thinking on the **HUMALOGY®** scale is a report in the Wall Street Journal (WSJ) about a large global insurance company's use of artificial intelligence (AI) to improve (optimize) the claim adjudication process. The report revealed that the large number of emails sent to customers being generated by AI are overall more empathetic and less accusatory than human-written ones. "When these emails used to go out, even though we had standards and so on, they would include a lot of insurance jargon. They weren't very empathetic. Claims agents would get frustrated, and so it wasn't necessarily great communication" said Allstate Chief Information Officer Zulfi Jeevanjee, as reported by WSJ journalist Ms. Isabelle Bousquette, author of the report.

As organizations deploy more AI and Generative AI (GenAI) solutions that provide substitution of human activity, the employees of organizations will need guidance and assistance on what the change means to their job responsibilities and their relationships with others, including employees, suppliers and customers. This idea of including relationships assessments as part of an OCM method for stakeholder management merits a thoughtful design and use, as well as messaging and training for employees whose roles and job tasks may be replaced or augmented by AI. In the year 2025 these realities need to be considered and included in any OCM strategy and plan. The application of **HUMALOGY®** can provide the insights and ideation required for the change and the desired outcome in creating value for the organization and its stakeholders.

Organizational Change Management Insights

The root causes of poor stakeholder adoption in change initiatives are twofold: (1) program and project planning often focus too much on technology, neglecting the behavioral and cultural factors that impede user adoption, and (2) accountabilities for managing change and achieving business outcomes are not clearly defined or planned in advance.

Persuading people to change requires a "soft," empathetic approach to keep them engaged and motivated. However, "soft" should not be mistaken for easy. Managing the people side of change is demanding, requiring comfort and competence in dealing with uncertainty, ambiguity, purpose, and conflict.

In today's business world, transformation and change are becoming the new normal. While this may make people more open to change, specific organizational changes need to be carefully planned, communicated, orchestrated, and managed. Agility and continuous improvement are valuable traits but can become volatile if change is not properly managed.

To ensure successful change initiatives and maximize value, focus on the emotional, behavioral, cultural, and relational factors that foster resistance and hinder adoption. Make Organizational Change Management (OCM) as integral to the process as the change itself. Foster a culture that is proactive and receptive to OCM by embedding it into the company's DNA. Institutionalize OCM by factoring it into project ideation and managing it throughout the project lifecycle, even after the project ends, for monitoring and measurement.

Equip project leaders with the tools necessary to influence and support change across the enterprise. Effective OCM demands an actionable toolkit to plant the seeds for organizational change. The success of this depends on the company's historical view of change, its values and culture, and its readiness for change. With the right tools, processes, and messaging, the OCM team can become the hub of organizational change, helping teams consistently achieve success during and after projects.

Learning from Greatness

One of my life's greatest moments was meeting General Colin Powell, twice. We met in an Operation Desert Storm theater of operations. It was a surreal and defining moment to meet the general while in uniform. Years later, following my departure from EDS I found myself at a dinner table during a black-tie gala in Chicago. I was a late addition, pinch hitting for one of our firm's partners who was unable to attend the event. Although I was aware our firm was a platinum sponsor, I was not aware I would be sitting at the table with the event's guest keynote speaker, General Colin Powell. Our conversation that evening is one I won't forget, even twenty-some years later. I had been a student of General Powell's Thirteen Rules of Leadership in my early days at EDS. Rule Thirteen is "Perpetual optimism is a force multiplier." This means that a leader's unwavering optimism can create an exponential positive impact and significantly boost their effectiveness and inspire others to achieve more than they otherwise would. It is the wise change leader who understands this and seeks to create it when leading change. For the times they are a-changin'. And so are we.

"If your time to you is worth savin'Then you better start swimmin'
Or you'll sink like a stone
For the times they are a-changin'."

- Bob Dylan

ABOUT THE AUTHOR

Robert Sheesley

Robert Sheesley is a strategically focused executive leader who leverages a blend of strategy, leadership, technology and organizational change navigation to consistently align organizational purpose and business capabilities with technology to drive high-impact outcomes. With experience in a variety of industries, including health care, pharmaceuticals, insurance, home services, and manufacturing, he specializes in strategy, private equity, mergers and acquisitions, digital transformation and start-up SaaS advisory. Robert is known for being a servant leader and a player-coach, building high performance teams. A U.S. Marine and Operation Desert Storm Veteran, Robert holds a Business Architecture certificate from DePaul University, Cyber Security Leadership and Enterprise Architecture certificates from Carnegie Mellon University, a TOGAF 9 Enterprise Architecture Certification from The Open Group, and a Merger and Acquisition Integration Expert Certificate from Pritchett, LP.

In his previous role as Chief Information Officer of private equity-backed Wrench Group, an industry leading home services consolidator, Robert was responsible for setting the digital and technology strategy, leading over thirty acquisition integrations across fourteen states, building a corporate technology and operations organization from concept to scale, and evolving the information, infrastructure, security, data privacy and computing platforms that enabled Wrench Group's historic growth, landing the company on the Inc 5000 in 2021, placing in the top 60% of rankings. He is the recipient of the

HotTopic's 2024 Global CIO 100 award, ETS Solution's 2024 Servant Technology Concilium CIO of The Year award, 2023 Georgia CIO of The Year Orbie award, and Technology Association of Georgia (TAG) 2022 Digital Transformation Project of the Year award. He is a member of the Forbes Technology Council and serves on the Executive Advisory Council of Inspiredu Atlanta, the Business Advisory Council of the Eberly Business School at Indiana University and the Georgia State University's Robinson College of Business, Department of Computer Information Systems Board of Advisors.

Robert enjoys spending time with his wife Lanette and their German Shepherds, Delos and Doonagore, children Eden, McKenzie and Andrew, and family. He and Lanette are actively involved with Saint Martha Catholic Church in Sarasota. Robert enjoys travel, reading, golf, fishing, writing and theatre.

When You Grow

Natalie Salaiz-Padilla

I grew up in a small mountain community tucked in a national forest inside Kern County, California. In 1984, my parents moved us into the log cabin home they built from the ground up. My dad commuted to and from Los Angeles for work, two hours each way, while my mom homeschooled my big sister and me for the first few years of grammar school. The nearest city, Bakersfield, was about an hour away. Mom would pack us into the car for hour-long trips to shop at Food 4 Less, Pic N Save, ACE Hardware, Michaels, and JoAnn Fabrics for clothing patterns. Being a single-income family, my mom taught herself many trades to make our home the best on less. She dedicated her life to us, with the utmost love and sweetness, sewing our clothes, baking cookies, bread, and pizza dough from scratch. I have vivid memories of her sitting on our deck, sipping on her freshly brewed sun tea, cutting pictures from *Better Homes & Gardens* magazines to inspire ideas for her garden and our home while my sister and I played in our fort in the forest. She fueled our imaginations with storytelling and adventure; she taught us to be industrious and clever. My mom's work ethic, even to this day, is something I have always admired. My mom supplemented our income by taking on side jobs, wallpapering homes or reupholstering furniture, all self-taught. She was, and still is, the kind of mom who could turn a handful of rocks into a collection of magical keepsakes. Her creativity breathed life into our daily existence.

The house that built me – 1984

My dad, likely exhausted from a day of work and his commute, never let it show. He had two little girls waiting by the window to watch his car pull in the drive. The moment he walked through the door, he was greeted by the fresh smell of a home-cooked meal (compliments of mom), two little girls ready for his time and attention, and a wife likely ready for a bit of R&R. Dad gave in to our every request. He played "Fishin' Time" with us, built epic pillow forts, played Old Maid, checkers, and Go Fish, fed the porch racoons for our entertainment, and spent hours coloring with us. He taught us that coloring people green with purple hair and outside the lines was a totally valid art form. He chopped our firewood, cut down our Christmas trees, took us searching for horned toads at *Lizard Gulch* (a place I later realized he had named himself), dabbled in pheasant rearing and even barbecued roadkill rattlesnake after an afternoon hunt—yes, it tastes like chicken. He taught us how to tough it out through our scrapes and bruises, that mayonnaise gets tree sap off your hands, and quitting is only an option once a job is done. Without fail, every winter, he'd put out a bowl, collect the fresh fallen snow, and make the sweetest fluffiest batch of snow ice cream! He was, and still is, the perfect combination of a tenderly tough girl dad who I knew I could count on no matter what.

My parents created the sweetest memories in a totally off-the-grid, small-town-living type of way. I look back on my childhood with sincere gratitude and recognize that I am who I am today because of how I was raised. My values and worldview that inform my leadership style emerged from these sweet, simple, and industrious times. Technology was nearly absent from our lives, aside from an antique rotary dial phone, a TV, and a VCR. When I was almost eight, we moved away from the mountains. At the time it was a devastating move. I like to remind my parents that it was the day they "ruined my life." Dramatic much? Yes. However, the transition from the quiet simplicity of Kern County to the much faster pace of Riverside County was a shock, to say the least. I could have never imagined where I would end up or how my life would evolve. My mom and dad created such a perfect childhood for me that it was all I ever wanted. I hoped to grow up and recreate the same for my own family. My vision was to return to my childhood home, buy it back, and be the exact version of my mom for my own kids. I held on so tightly to this that I was not open to any alternatives.

If you had asked me 32 years ago where I thought I would be, what I wanted to be when I grew up, or what my ambitions were—I would never have imagined working in an Information Technology department, let alone serving as the Associate Vice President.

My Unexpected Path to IT Leadership

I didn't own a computer until I was 27 years old. For perspective, as I write this, I am now 40. Even after moving to the city, my family didn't have cable TV or internet until my early 20s. I grew up in an era of emerging technology but in a home of simplicity. We simply were not interested in technology in our everyday lives. As such, my path to the IT industry and IT leadership is quite unintentional and more on the side of happenstance.

In my late teens and early 20s, I was a flightless bird with zero direction. My young mutiny can be a whole how-not-to book in and of itself, so just know, I was a hot mess. College didn't interest me. There was not a single hobby, job, or idea that I didn't quit before it had a chance to flourish. I hopped from job to job—fast food, coffee shops, retail, bridal boutiques, wedding planning, makeup artistry, and hairstyling. I am a three-time beauty school dropout. I was stuck. At 19, with hot pink streaks in my black hair, my aunt, an Admissions Director, offered me a temp office job. Little did I know that would be the beginning of a 20-year journey of growth, learning, and self-discovery. The temporary work turned into five years of position surfing at the University. I eventually landed in a position reporting to Dr. Denise (NeeCee) Cornish. I consider myself a bit of a rescue.

NeeCee changed the trajectory of my adult life. You know the saying, people don't quit jobs, just bad bosses? I have vowed to follow NeeCee to the ends of the Earth! When I interviewed for a job as an Administrative Assistant in the IT department, my knowledge of technology was limited to a few last-minute Google searches of basic IT terms and concepts that I crammed before my interview. I made it through my first interview wondering whether it was enough, and whether I did enough. In the middle of my workday, I received a call back offering me a second interview. To say I was elated is an understatement. To show up for my second interview, I told my boss that my grandma was sick, and I had to leave immediately.

Now, I live by the standard that you never lie or place illness upon a loved one. At the time, my grandma was in hospice, so it wasn't *not* true, but I certainly pushed the ethical boundary. I was determined to do whatever it took to get the job, even if it meant risking my current job. As a disheveled 24-year-old, I happened to have a car trunk full of clothes, shoes, odds and ends. I was pulling out all the stops, and willing to do whatever it took to land this job in IT. I pieced together the most professional outfit I could from what I had in the trunk, and drenched myself in perfume to mask the potential car smell. I walked into NeeCee's office, not knowing what to expect. I sat down, took a deep breath, and she offered me the position. I can remember the sigh of relief and feeling of being overcome by emotion—joy, excitement, and anticipation. I told her, *"I want to cry or hug you."* She said, "Well, don't cry. There's no crying in baseball." I promised her I would be a hard worker, committed to learning, and would never make her regret taking a chance on me. We hugged as I left her office. That day, the trajectory of my life changed forevermore. She took a chance on me then—and every day since.

Embracing the Uncomfortable

There is something serendipitous about stepping into a space where you feel completely unqualified. With a bit of grit, it forces you to swim. The choices we have in these moments of uncertainty are to retreat or push forward. Having a hunger to learn, I pushed forward, living by the aphorism "fake it until you make it." I still did not believe I had "IT" or leadership potential. At the time, I saw my future as either-or: I could either be a great mother or have a career—I did not believe that I could have or be both. I entered the IT world seeing it as a temporary means to an end.

Catalysts to change can come in unexpected channels. For me it was someone else's change that prompted my own. NeeCee decided to go back to school for her doctorate while leading a 20-person team and raising two young daughters. She stayed up late, woke up early, and somehow made it all work. To me, she made it look effortless. I'm sure if you ask her, she'd have a different narrative. That space in time shifted my entire perspective. I realized that leadership and growth, like life, is about intentional balance, not sacrifice.

At 32, I took her encouragement to heart and enrolled in college. Now eight years later, I have graduated summa cum laude with a Bachelor's in Communication. After a month off, I re-enrolled to start my Master's in Communication with an emphasis in Education. I graduated with a 4.0 amid a worldwide pandemic and a high-risk pregnancy with my third baby. Today, I am on the precipice of earning my PhD in Cognitive Psychology. I am a first-generation college graduate, a mom of three beautiful children, a dog mom of two, a wife to my best friend, and a leader of an extraordinary team of technology professionals.

Six Leadership Lessons from an Unconventional Journey

If there's one thing I have learned, it's that leadership isn't about titles—it's about impact. My journey to leadership wasn't straightforward. Along the way, I picked up valuable lessons that shaped the leader I am today. Trusting the process and being open to being moldable, accepting feedback, and keeping a growth mindset is essential to earning a role in leadership.

1. Say Yes Before You Feel Ready

I wasn't qualified for my first IT job, but I took it because I knew I could learn and would be open to being molded. There is something beautiful about being moldable. Having an openness to learning and a willingness to admit you are not the expert creates a space of endless possibility.

Growth happens when we say *yes* before we feel ready. Sometimes, you must bet on yourself before anyone else does. And sometimes, someone else bets on you before you bet on yourself. Investing in your growth and pushing yourself toward excellence is one of the best things you can do for yourself. Keep learning. Go back to school. Work toward the degree you didn't think was possible. Take extra classes. Read books. Listen to podcasts. Steal time from the leaders you admire the most. Watch others with the intent to learn. I studied NeeCee's every move. I watched how she handled difficult situations. I learned by mimicking and then adapting to create my own leadership style.

We can tend to have tunnel vision or limit ourselves to what we think should be our path. Many factors are at play in what we *think* we should be or do. Having someone who can open your perspective and show you how to think beyond norms can put you in places you never thought possible.

2. Find a Mentor (or Be One)

NeeCee saw something in me that I hadn't seen yet in myself. Great leaders don't just lead; they lift others up.. If you're lucky enough to have a mentor, listen. And when you're in a position to mentor, don't hesitate to invest in others. Don't fall into the trap of thinking you don't have something to offer. Our journeys are meant to be shared. You never know who they may help.

3. Embrace Discomfort as a Catalyst for Growth

Every defining moment in my career stemmed from discomfort. From walking into an IT department with no experience to juggling motherhood, leadership, and a PhD Every challenge stretches me into something greater. Growth and discomfort are inseparable, but so exciting and worth it when you lean into it, exist in it, and especially don't fight it.

4. Leadership is About People, Not Power

In IT, people may assume leadership is about managing systems and technology. But leadership is about serving our people. We have been entrusted with a team, a vision, and a mission. The best leaders serve, listen, and create environments where others can thrive. I am nothing without my team. I recently took a class where we were told to "become experts in leadership, but generalists in technology." That really resonated with me because often we can fall into the clutches of feeling like we must know everything to be the best. I actually think it's the not knowing everything that propels us to excellence. It's having a growth mindset and humility to serve alongside our teams, to empower, not command.

5. Don't Stop, Don't Give Up

When my daughter was 5, she used to sing this song "Don't stop, don't give up" every time she'd get frustrated learning something new. Her sweet resilience is something I hear in my head every time I feel the weight of entering another uncharted territory. My fight-or-flight response goes straight to fly. Fly far; fly fast; fly away! Leaning into challenges and building a network of people you trust to support you is pivotal to success. I worked my way through several roles in IT. I have a mentor who sees my potential and challenges me to keep reaching.

Not every role was an immediate yes. Sometimes, there were no's, delays, and conditions I needed to meet to advance to the next level. I started as an Administrative Assistant, then worked my way through varying roles: Operations Coordinator, Business Systems Analyst, Assistant Director, Director of Enterprise Applications and Databases, and Interim Assistant Vice President of IT. All of which led to my current role of Associate Vice President of IT. The key is to not give up or stop if the target keeps moving.

6. Find Your Balance

Comparison is a catalyst to self-deprecation. How "Samantha" is the room-mom, President of the PTA, does 6 am Pilates, Saturday brunch, Tuesday night Bingo, meal preps, has Johnny potty trained by 9 months old, Susy in travel dance club, is fully dressed and functional for morning drop-off is none of my business. I love that for her! I give that example because those are things that used to make me feel like I wasn't enough. Now I'm in awe of the parents out there who do these kinds of things so effortlessly. Like, share your secret, friend!

We can force ourselves into other people's molds because from the outside looking in, that person is doing better than us. We all have a unique journey in life. At some point, we may feel like we're blowing it somewhere or everywhere at once. Truth is, we are not perfect beings capable of giving our undivided attention to every task or ask that befalls us. It can feel like we're winning at one and failing at another. In reality, there are moments where we can't show up. Whether it be the social event of the year that could really boost your network or the spring 2nd grade field trip to the farm—we must weigh and measure where we spend our time.

Give yourself grace. Have those important conversations with the people in your life about what it means for you to be successful in your career and successful at home. Establish boundaries and stick to them. Forgive yourself when you don't get it right all the time. Ask for forgiveness from others.

If I could go back and talk to my younger self, I'd say: *"It's okay not to have it all figured out. Just keep saying* yes." My career has taken me places I never thought I'd go. I've had the opportunity to travel, share my story and experience, and learn alongside industry leaders I'm in awe of. I continue to have some real pinch-me, how-did-I-get-here moments, to say the least. The unexpected becomes a reality when we remove preconceptions and plans that we *think* we *must* follow. It all became possible with the help of someone who took a chance on me, and once I abandoned the all-or-nothing mentality and accepted help and guidance.

I am forever grateful to my parents for a childhood rooted in simplicity and resilience—two things that have made me adaptable in every stage of life. To NeeCee, thank you for taking a chance on a girl without a dream and creating a space where I could grow beyond my own boundaries.

P.S. Mom and Dad, when you read this, thank you for *not* ruining my life.

Who says you can't go home? Pine Mountain Club, California, 2024

ABOUT THE AUTHOR

Natalie Salaiz-Padilla

Natalie Salaiz-Padilla is the Associate Vice President of Information Technology at Western University of Health Sciences, where she leads transformative initiatives that enhance academic excellence, operational efficiency, and innovation. She has successfully developed and executed a multi-year strategic IT plan aligned with university goals, optimized software licensing to achieve over $250K in annual savings, and implemented a unified campus-wide communication platform to streamline access and improve user experience.

Natalie is recognized for reshaping IT culture through a human-centered leadership model grounded in transparency, trust, and professional development. Passionate about people-first leadership, she thrives on solving complex challenges with empathy and aligning strategy with meaningful impact.

A strong communicator, Natalie creates space for others to feel seen, valued, and connected to purpose in their work. Her leadership is defined by how she elevates others and fosters a culture where people and innovation thrive side by side. She is known for building trust across all levels of the organization and for her distinctive leadership style—a blend of grit and grace rooted in purpose.

Outside of IT leadership, Natalie finds joy in life's simple and soulful moments—exploring mountain trails, collecting seashells, painting, and getting lost in true crime podcasts. She's a proud mom of three, a devoted wife, and a lifelong adventurer who seeks heart and perspective into every facet of life.

Her guiding philosophy: Where people thrive, purpose drives, and leadership leaves a legacy.

When Your Stakeholders Change

Ed DePrimo

In today's dynamic business environment, organizational changes are a constant reality. Whether through restructuring, acquisitions, divestitures, or leadership transitions, these changes often shape the trajectory of careers. For senior IT leaders, the ability to navigate these shifts effectively is not just a skill—it's a critical factor in career advancement. Success in this arena can open doors to new opportunities and growth, while failure can lead to stagnation.

While technical skills, project management know-how, financial savvy, teamwork, and strong communication are all essential parts of leadership, nothing carries more weight than your ability to manage relationships with key stakeholders. After all, opportunities often come from those who control access to them. No matter how capable or visible you are, you won't be invited to the table if you haven't built those relationships.

Success in leadership depends on earning the trust and support of others, both quietly and directly. Without it, even your most carefully planned initiatives can stall. But with it, you gain momentum—and often, access to the kinds of opportunities that can truly move your organization (and your career) forward.

IT leaders operate within a community that includes both technical experts and business stakeholders, each wielding varying degrees of influence and power. Recognizing this and understanding the critical role others play in shaping your career is essential to your long-term success.

While understanding the technical landscape is an important part of any IT leader's journey, the real challenge often lies in navigating the world of business stakeholders. These are people with long histories, deep-rooted connections, and complex dynamics that may not be immediately visible to an incoming IT leader.

To many in this group, IT is still seen as a cost center—necessary, but secondary. Some may feel intimidated by technology, viewing it as something that slows them down rather than helps them reach their goals. Gaining their trust and respect can take time and patience, especially in environments where relationships run deep, and the players frequently change.

Having experienced 10 executive team transitions across five different companies, I've gained unique insights into the nuances of managing stakeholders during times of organizational change. Additionally, my four years as an independent consultant, collaborating with over 20 different executive teams, provided me with invaluable experience in adapting to various corporate cultures, communication styles, and business priorities.

Based on these experiences, here are five key strategies for building meaningful relationships with stakeholders and advancing your career through organizational change.

Establish Rapport Early

Building personal connections with stakeholders isn't just helpful—it's essential. When you're new to an organization, make it a priority to spend time with key stakeholders one-on-one. Listen to their stories, understand their pain points, and show genuine interest in their goals and challenges. Look for quick wins—small actions that ease frustrations or solve simple problems. These early efforts can generate goodwill and build momentum for stronger collaboration down the road.

Keep the conversations regular, candid, and two-way. That ongoing dialogue is what keeps priorities aligned and relationships strong.

Expand Your Network

Don't stop at your immediate stakeholders. Ask them who else you should meet within their teams or departments—and take the time to build relationships with those individuals as well. Keep your primary stakeholders in the loop, of course, but also be discreet and respectful in how you build trust with others. When you show up, follow through, and deliver results, word gets around. Over time, you'll develop a reputation as someone who understands the business and gets things done.

Establish a Regular Cadence

Take the lead in setting up recurring one-on-one meetings with your key stakeholders to stay aligned and keep the lines of communication open. These can be virtual or in-person—whatever works best—but consistency matters. Meetings will inevitably get bumped or rescheduled, so be proactive about rebooking them. Always come prepared with meaningful updates or progress on shared goals. Think of these meetings not as reporting sessions, but as opportunities to align on priorities, troubleshoot roadblocks, and strategize for what's ahead—both in the short term and the long run.

Keep Them Engaged

Effective engagement has to be a two-way street. If your conversations become one-sided—with you simply providing updates—your stakeholder's interest will fade over time. Keep them actively involved in matters that fall within their scope, and seek their perspective when it adds value. While you should handle issues independently when possible, don't hesitate to tap into their expertise when guidance is needed. That level of collaboration builds trust and keeps the relationship strong.

Communication

You've likely heard it before, but it's worth repeating: communication is everything—and in this space, it *will* be tested. Here are two recommendations that have served me well over the years.

First, adapt to your stakeholder's communication style. Are they storytellers, or do they prefer short, direct statements? Do they organize their thoughts with bullet points, or do they lean into big-picture strategy? Do they share personal anecdotes or stick strictly to business? Pay close attention and mirror their style. This will help you stay in sync.

Second, talk less. Use your time with them to truly listen and absorb their insights. When you do speak, be clear and concise, and focus on what's relevant and timely. Personal stories and small talk can help build rapport, but keep it light and purposeful.

In Summary

These practices—refined over years of navigating complex leadership environments—are essential for effective stakeholder management, especially during times of change. When you master the art of building trust, staying connected, and adapting your approach, you position yourself for sustained success and meaningful career growth, no matter how turbulent the landscape becomes.

Ed DePrimo is a seasoned business IT executive with wide-ranging experience assisting companies reach their next level of growth, scalability, and maturity. He specializes in enabling IT transformations, governing capital investment cycles, developing empowered team-based organizations, implementing cyber security programs, and obtaining financial synergies from acquisitions. Ed is certified as a Qualified Technology Executive with a successful history of guiding companies through their cybersecurity journey.

ABOUT THE AUTHOR

Ed DePrimo

Ed DePrimo has held senior IT leadership roles, including CIO for several global organizations, where he consistently built and led high-performing teams. These teams were grounded in a clear purpose: delivering high-quality, value-added services while exceeding expectations and commitments.

Under Ed's leadership, IT has been a catalyst for transformational change—driving global ERP implementations, deploying business-driven best-of-breed solutions, and significantly improving service-level performance across key operational metrics.

A committed servant leader, Ed believes in sharing power, putting people first, and creating an environment where individuals are empowered to grow and thrive. His leadership style has been shaped by real-world experience and a deep appreciation for the human side of team success.

Ed's core belief is that everyone has the potential to achieve more. By leading from that perspective, he has helped countless professionals reach career milestones they once thought were out of reach.

When Charting an Unconventional Path

Kimberley Wheaton-Fuerst

My journey to becoming an IT Director did not follow the traditional path you might expect. I didn't begin by studying computer science, nor did I immerse myself in a typical tech-focused education. Instead, my career choices were shaped by personal interests, unexpected opportunities, and a willingness to embrace change. While unconventional, these experiences filled my toolbox with the skills I use each and every day.

Early Lesson in Leadership and Resilience

Who I was as a child has a lot to do with who I am today. I was the little girl who made friends with everyone. I didn't care about skin color, family background, or gender. I gravitated toward those who weren't part of the "in" crowd. People often described me as a natural leader—whatever that truly meant. What I did know was that I often felt like an outcast, different from everyone else. I attended four high schools, dropping out repeatedly because I never quite fit in. When I finally graduated at 19, it was the early '90s, and I faced a decision about what to pursue next. I remember weighing two very different paths: Social Work or Operations and Production Management. When a college counselor at Centennial College told me the Operations program had a ratio of one woman to every 10 men, that sealed the deal. As a young woman with a bit of a defiant streak, I thought, *Why not break into that space.*

Continuous Learning: A Constant Companion

I enrolled in the co-op program, which turned out to be one of the best decisions I ever made. The combination of academic studies and hands-on industry placements gave me valuable, real-world experience. By the time I graduated, my toolbox was stocked with both academic knowledge and practical skills, and I was fortunate enough to have three job offers waiting for me. I chose to begin as a production planner at a manufacturing firm that produced broadcasting equipment. While I enjoyed the work and picked up some of the basics, I quickly began to crave more dynamic challenges.

I wanted to keep growing, and I recognized the importance of building business acumen. To satisfy that hunger, I enrolled part-time in the Bachelor of Commerce program at Ryerson University. At the same time, my professional role was evolving. I became a facilitator of process improvements, which expanded my reach across the organization and helped me hone key soft skills, such as collaboration, coordination, and change management.

After a year of working and attending class, I was given the chance to take my new academic skills and apply them within my organization. I seized the opportunity and moved into purchasing as a buyer, focusing on PC boards and electronic components. I continued to grow my business knowledge and sharpened my skills in vendor management. Two years later, a Purchasing Manager at ClearNet (later acquired by TELUS) approached me about shifting into the telecommunications sector. This time, I was responsible for buying equipment like batteries and antennas.

Teaching: A Newfound Passion

These roles helped me develop stronger negotiation skills and refine how I worked with people. I went on to earn a CSCMP Designation in Supply Chain Management, a milestone that opened another unexpected door: teaching. I began lecturing in supply chain courses at Centennial, Seneca, and Humber Colleges. Teaching adult learners and newcomers to Canada was deeply rewarding. It wasn't just about sharing knowledge; it was about helping people shape their careers, improve their résumés, and find the confidence to move forward. Seeing how education and encouragement could truly change lives left a lasting impression on me.

Stepping Boldly Into IT

When TELUS acquired ClearNet, I had built a solid reputation for getting things done and collaborating effectively with diverse teams. This caught the attention of the IT Department, which needed a project coordinator to assist with contract management and project status reporting. Although I didn't have a strong technical background, I stepped into the role with confidence, relying on my adaptability and willingness to learn. It proved to be the gateway I needed into the world of technology. Around the same time, I graduated from Ryerson with my B.Comm. degree, but I knew my learning journey wasn't over. I had become fascinated by the field of project management and decided to pursue my PMP designation. After two more years of study, I earned the certification, which helped me move into the role of Project Manager II at TELUS.

In this new role, I managed projects aimed at improving software development efficiency. Surprisingly, my background in supply chain proved invaluable. Skills like process improvement, resource management, and stakeholder engagement translated seamlessly across disciplines. I designed workflows and collaborated closely with IT and development teams, identifying synergies and creating solutions that improved both timelines and outcomes.

Wearing Many Hats: Expanding Technical Expertise

Eventually, I felt ready for another adventure and joined a small software company as a Senior Project Manager. With only fourteen employees, everyone wore multiple hats. I established project management processes from the ground up and worked closely with the development team, further sharpening my technical skills.

Reinventing Processes at SmartCentres

After a year, a new opportunity surfaced: a Process Improvement Manager role at SmartCentre REIT, a real estate development firm. This was yet another industry pivot, but I welcomed the challenge. Drawing on my business skills, software development experience, and process improvement background, I discovered innovative ways to replace paper forms with mobile applications—what we now refer to as digital transformation. With the support of the visionary VP who hired me, I pushed my creative boundaries and became the developer of these user-friendly apps, even without a formal technical background. I understood the importance of simplicity, usability, and a positive user experience, and I applied those principles to every solution I implemented.

Finding Purpose at York Regional Police

Three years into my time at SmartCentres, I came across an opening for an IT Project Leader at York Regional Police. The opportunity to support my local police service intrigued me, so I applied and was offered the position. In this role, I led one of the most significant technical shifts in modern policing: the development of an electronic note-taking application for officers. I also managed the deployment of more than 1,400 cell phones across the force. This work brought together technology, change management, and community service, and I truly embraced the challenge.

Reaching the Director's Chair

Then came the opportunity to apply for the IT Director role. I went for it and got it. Today, I bring together all the varied threads of my career:

technology, people management, process efficiency, strategic thinking, and continuous improvement. It's been a non-traditional path, but one full of valuable lessons. Every step—from choosing to study Operations and Production Management, to buying antennas, to shifting into process improvement and technology—shaped me into the agile, curious, and empathetic leader I am today.

If my journey teaches anything, it's that you don't need to start with a coding boot camp or a computer science degree to become an IT Director. I built my career on adaptability, curiosity, resilience, and a constant desire to learn. I embraced human connection, leaned into challenges, and consistently invested in my own growth.

The Hard Truth Behind Success

My journey hasn't always been easy. There have been moments when workplace politics tested me, and more than once, I found myself in tears—frustrated, angry, or simply overwhelmed. As a woman, I've experienced times when my voice was dismissed or unheard, and I've had to push harder to be recognized. Some of my most valuable growth has come from missteps, difficult decisions, and the lessons that followed. And while I've grown in confidence, there's still a part of me that feels unsure at times. It's a reminder that personal growth is ongoing.

Parting Words for Fellow Adventurers

To anyone reading my story: be kind, be courageous, be curious, be honest, and above all, be true to yourself. Smile in the face of challenges. Draw strength from your past achievements when you begin to doubt your abilities. And remember, there's no single, straight path to leadership. Sometimes, it's the winding road that leads to the richest experiences. Good luck on your own adventure.

ABOUT THE AUTHOR

Kimberley Wheaton-Fuerst

Kimberley Wheaton-Fuerst is an accomplished IT Director based in Newmarket, Ontario, with a breadth of experience across agile and waterfall project management methodologies. Currently serving at York Regional Police, she has spearheaded projects such as the implementation of an Electronic Notes application and the distribution of over 1,000 smartphones to the YRP members in which she received the Chief Of Police Award in 2024.

Her expertise in quality improvement, change management, and financial reporting is complemented by her extensive skills in client management and team building. Kimberley's background includes roles at Smart Centres REIT as a Process Improvement Manager and as a Project Manager at TELUS Communications, where she enhanced operational value through strategic project delivery and process innovation.

Kimberley holds a Bachelor of Business Management from Ryerson University and a Business Diploma from Centennial College. She is certified in Business Process Management, Six Sigma, Scrum, and Project Management. Kimberley has also contributed to the academic field as a part-time instructor at several colleges, receiving a "Teaching Excellence Award" in 2015 for her work at Centennial College.

When Culture Eats Strategy, Politics Is the Knife and Fork

Dallan Elk

Growing up, I made it my mission to instill a love of learning in my son. Along the way, I took a few creative liberties—like the day I told him that a very smart man, Dr. Michael Porter, once said, "Culture eats strategy for breakfast." It was a harmless fib, meant to spark curiosity and start a conversation. To my surprise, it worked a little too well.

The phrase resonated deeply with him. Suddenly, my son—who was as passionate about Marvel superheroes and Braves baseball as any typical 8-year-old—developed a fascination with Porter's business strategies. His roster of heroes expanded to include not only Spider-Man and Chipper Jones but also Harvard Business School professors. We often talked about how this deceptively simple idea—culture trumping strategy—applied far beyond the boardroom. It applied to his soccer team, his school, and even our home life. Culture, I explained, is the fabric that holds any group together, dictating how people interact and what they value. Strategy might set the direction, but culture decides whether anyone actually follows through.

By the time he was 12, my son was writing speeches for Future Business Leaders of America on concepts like Shared Value and emailing Dr. Porter directly for feedback. Let me pause here to acknowledge my relief that Dr. Porter, likely drowning in correspondence from aspiring business leaders twice my son's age, never responded. Why? Because it would have exposed my little oopsie.

You see, it wasn't Michael Porter who coined the famous phrase "Culture eats strategy for breakfast." That credit belongs to Peter Drucker. I'm not sure what would've been worse—admitting my mistake or hearing my son gleefully lecture me about it for years to come. Either way, I decided to let sleeping dogs lie and instead celebrate the odd yet inspirational impact both Drucker and Porter had on my family.

And so, as a tribute to them both—and perhaps as a small act of penance for misattributing the quote—I offer this chapter. It's a reflection on my own experiences with that simple, powerful truth: *culture eats strategy for breakfast.* With one small addition of my own: *Politics is the knife and fork.*

Culture can define the success or failure of a team, company, or any group working toward a common goal. But it's often politics—the hidden agendas, personal egos, and unspoken rules—that determine how that culture functions in real life. In the pages that follow, I'll share stories of how culture, strategy, and politics collided, sometimes with surprising results, sometimes with predictable disasters, but always with a lesson attached. To protect both the innocent and the guilty (and to keep this entertaining), I won't follow a strict chronological timeline. But like any good story, I'll start at the beginning.

Mr. Spock – A Lesson in Trust, Transparency, and Resilience

Early in my career, I joined a small but ambitious company. Long before *SaaS* became a buzzword, this was a product-driven organization. But its true strength wasn't in its offerings—it was in its people. From day one, I was awestruck by the extraordinary talent surrounding me, from my coworkers to the leadership.

One leader in particular, whom I'll call Mr. Spock, embodied the qualities of trust, transparency, and resilience. An Englishman with a calm, measured demeanor, he led the company through the tumultuous dot-com bubble burst. Under his guidance, we faced two rounds of layoffs, delayed paychecks, and countless challenges. Yet, despite these hardships, we rallied behind him. We trusted him.

Trust, the Foundation of Leadership

Mr. Spock wasn't a developer, but he deeply understood the nuances of good coding and respected the craft. He was genuine, transparent, and made every team member feel valued. He cultivated a culture of cohesion by hiring individuals who fit not just the job but the company's ethos. He also had a knack for incentivizing us to push through long hours—often in creative ways (many of which involved strong coffee and the occasional pint). But his most remarkable achievement was breaking the paradox of trust: he trusted us, supported us, and earned our unwavering trust in return.

Transparency, the Pillar of Stability

What set Mr. Spock apart wasn't just his ability to communicate but the way he did so—with unflinching transparency. He believed that trust could only thrive in an environment where information wasn't hidden or manipulated. When layoffs were on the horizon, Mr. Spock didn't shield us from the reality. Instead, he called the team together, explained the reasons behind the difficult decisions, and outlined the company's objectives to avoid further losses. He made it clear that these measures, as painful as they were, were about ensuring the company's survival.

When paychecks were delayed, he didn't leave us guessing or allow rumors to fester. He informed us in advance, giving us time to prepare. He assured us that if anyone had immediate financial needs, they could come to him for help. This level of honesty turned what could have been an atmosphere of panic into one of understanding and solidarity.

Later, we discovered the extent of his transparency and sacrifice. During the company's toughest times, Mr. Spock voluntarily took significant pay cuts and delayed his own compensation far beyond what was asked of the team. This act of selflessness wasn't just a gesture—it was proof of his commitment to us.

A Culture of Trust and Resilience

Mr. Spock's leadership created an environment where trust and transparency were not just values but daily practices. His openness about the company's struggles and his willingness to share hard truths made us feel like partners in the journey, not just employees. He reinforced this culture by consistently communicating both challenges and successes. If the company hit a milestone, we celebrated together. If we fell short, we understood why and how we would move forward. This approach kept us engaged and inspired us to give our best, even during the darkest days.

Conclusion

Mr. Spock's leadership was a masterclass in integrity, transparency, and resilience. By fostering open communication and leading with authenticity, he built a culture of trust that empowered us to persevere through uncertainty. His ability to share both the good and the bad without hesitation created a sense of unity that few organizations achieve. I'll always be grateful to Mr. Spock for showing us that true leadership isn't about avoiding adversity—it's about facing it head-on with honesty, trust, and unwavering commitment to your team.

The Hero – a Leadership Lesson in Resilience

For a time, I worked at a company where our flagship product—a vital revenue driver—was riddled with defects. Customers were furious, and the team was caught in a brutal cycle of rushing development to meet revenue goals, which only introduced more defects and exacerbated cash flow issues. Fixing the underlying problems required time we did not have, and leadership was unwilling to slow down development to address the root cause.

Amid this chaos, there was one person who stood out: my leader, The Hero. He oversaw all product-related teams and was the only one in senior leadership bold enough to challenge the status quo and call for a change to break the destructive cycle.

While others in leadership were consumed with political maneuvering and quick fixes, The Hero made an unpopular but courageous decision: he instructed the team to take two sprints to focus solely on fixing the most critical issues. At first glance, two sprints seemed insignificant, but for us, it was transformative. Knowing that someone was willing to fight for us galvanized the team.

Under his leadership, we came together with renewed purpose. We achieved our best-ever burndown rate, worked weekends, and even managed to squeeze in an additional sprint. Through it all, The Hero was with us every step of the way—caffeinating us, feeding us, and keeping morale high. He demonstrated that leadership is not just about strategy; it's about being in the trenches with your team and inspiring them to rise above adversity.

Lesson 1

A great leader makes the hard call and champions long-term solutions, even when it's unpopular. They create an environment and culture in which they can inspire their teams to rally together, reducing short-term pain to achieve lasting progress.

The Fallout

Despite the team's success, The Hero's willingness to challenge the status quo ultimately cost him. Two months later, he was terminated—a stark reminder of the dysfunction at the senior leadership level. The decision to remove him spoke volumes about the company's unwillingness to address its deeper cultural issues.

Lesson 2

Cultural change cannot succeed if dysfunction starts at the top. Without a leadership team willing to prioritize the long-term health of the organization over short-term optics, even the best efforts will falter.

Lasting Inspiration

Working under The Hero was a reminder of what true leadership looks like. It's not about avoiding conflict or maintaining popularity but about standing up for what's right and inspiring your team to achieve the impossible. Even in his absence, the lessons he left behind continue to resonate: great leaders push for meaningful change, lead with courage, and create a culture where teams can thrive—even in the face of adversity.

The Good Old Boys – a Leadership Lesson in Disguise

For a time, I worked at a company where three salesmen held the top leadership roles, ranging from President to Director. Informally, they were known as 'The Southern Gentleman,' 'The Father,' and 'The Fool.' Each of them shaped the company culture in ways that undermined the organization, and their collective leadership style could best be described as "Good Old Boys." The favoritism, lack of trust, and general morale issues that followed were predictable, but what I learned from navigating this environment proved invaluable.

The Southern Gentleman

The most senior of the trio, The Southern Gentleman, was the charismatic architect of this leadership group. With his southern drawl, disarming smile, and knack for colorful euphemisms, he charmed clients and colleagues alike. His charisma created an atmosphere of admiration, but his leadership was disingenuous to those not in the inner circle—a group I was decidedly not part of. What complicated matters more was his virtual absence from the office. Rarely present, he spent most of his time traveling to meet clients, leaving a leadership vacuum in his wake. His absence made it hard to trust his ability to steer the company effectively, and instead, we mostly just tread water.

The Father

Second in command was The Father, a genuinely kind man who excelled at building personal relationships. He was empathetic and approachable, the kind of leader who cared deeply for his team—but like The Southern Gentleman, he was often absent, whether for work-related travel or family commitments. Employees appreciated his warmth, but his inconsistency left the organization floundering. His empathy couldn't compensate for his lack of hands-on leadership.

The Fool

Lastly, there was The Fool, the youngest and least experienced member of the trio. Elevated to the role of Director, it was painfully obvious he was out of his depth. Where The Southern Gentleman relied on charm and The Father on empathy, The Fool leaned on intimidation. He lacked the soft skills to inspire or manage effectively, often alienating employees with his abrasive demeanor.

Together, this trio represented a leadership structure built on personal relationships rather than competence. Their loyalty to one another overshadowed the needs of the company, creating a toxic environment. My own career felt like it had been thrust into Defcon 3 as I struggled to meet team goals amidst their short-sighted decisions and erratic organizational changes.

Finding the Lesson Amid the Chaos

At first, I was locked in constant battles with The Southern Gentleman and The Father. They saw me as an outsider to their "Good Old Boys" club, and it was clear we didn't share the same social belief system. I found myself frustrated by their actions and intent, which seemed more about preserving their clique than advancing the company. Then, a realization hit me: We clearly did not have a common goal. Even though they set my job responsibilities, their goals—immediate topline revenue—completely conflicted with mine. They wanted a "Yes Man," and I am not that. If I couldn't match their expectations, I needed to modify my approach to better align with their beliefs.

This was a turning point. With this insight, I adjusted my strategy:

- Align with their perception of value: I learned to frame my team's achievements in terms of revenue impact.
- Communicate clearly: I became more intentional in explaining how our work contributed to their bottom-line goals.
- Set expectations for the future: I positioned my team's value in ways they could understand and appreciate.

In short, they were suffering from Maslow's hammer, and until I explained how my strategic direction looked like a nail they were comfortable with, I couldn't succeed. By messaging directly to their goals instead of letting them infer the various company objectives, I was able to rebuild trust and improve my standing with leadership.

Just as things began to stabilize, however, The Southern Gentleman departed, leaving The Father to take on the most senior role. While his leadership style was familiar, The Fool was promoted—and the challenges of dealing with the trio intensified as they became a duo.

Navigating The Fool

With The Fool now elevated, my career moved to Defcon 2. His lack of experience was more glaring than ever, and his inability to recognize his own shortcomings made him particularly difficult to work with. Unlike his predecessors, The Fool didn't embrace the "trust but verify" principle that experienced leaders rely on. He demanded more proof, more explanations, and more hand-holding than the role warranted. Frustration mounted as The Father left the company, promoting The Fool into the senior position. I learned another key lesson:

Strategy relies on the best and brightest. In a toxic culture, the best and brightest are the first to depart. In such an environment, strategy has little chance of success. All the best people were out the door. Instead of recognizing the resource vacuum from the cultural cataclysm The Fool created, the blame for the inability to deliver fell squarely onto us, his leadership team.

What truly made The Fool foolish wasn't his inexperience—it was his inability to recognize and address his own shortcomings. Any attempts to fix the situation were met with public mockery and private dress-downs. Within a couple of months, The Fool was let go, leaving a broken culture in his wake. A great leader and teacher was needed to help bring it back together, if that was even possible.

The Takeaway

Working under The Southern Gentleman, The Father, and The Fool was anything but easy—at times, it felt downright abusive. Yet, amidst the dysfunction, I take comfort in knowing the lessons I learned were invaluable.

In a dysfunctional organization, the goals of individual leaders often diverge from the overarching goals of the company. This misalignment can make navigating such environments uniquely challenging, particularly in IT, where strategic initiatives typically require long-term focus. In these situations, understanding how leadership perceives immediate value becomes just as important—if not more so—than evaluating their actual competence.

By aligning your contributions to their short-term goals and demonstrating tangible value early on, you can begin to build trust. This trust becomes the foundation from which you can incrementally introduce and drive more significant, transformative changes over time. It's a delicate balance, but one that can pave the way for meaningful progress, even in the most dysfunctional settings.

In Closing

We've seen the good, the bad, and the downright ridiculous. Mr. Spock and The Hero reminded us that great leaders are like the Avengers of the workplace—trustworthy, transparent, and always ready to rally the team, even when the odds are stacked against them. They're the ones who keep the coffee flowing, the morale high, and the ship afloat, even when it feels like the ship is made of duct tape and hope.

And then… there were The Good Old Boys. Let's be real—there's nothing funny about that chapter. The Southern Gentleman, The Father, and The Fool were less of a leadership team and more of a cautionary tale. Favoritism, inconsistency, and a complete lack of self-awareness turned the workplace into a survival reality show. If leadership were a sport, they'd be the team that somehow managed to score points for the other side. It was tough, frustrating, and at times, downright demoralizing. But hey, if nothing else, they taught us what *not* to do—and sometimes, that's just as valuable.

So, what's the takeaway from all this? Leadership is messy. It's hard. It's occasionally absurd, often exhausting, and sometimes feels like herding cats. But it is also an opportunity to make a real difference—to build a culture where people feel valued to be courageous, craft a strategy that actually works, and navigate office politics without losing their sanity (or sense of humor).

In closing, let's remember that culture may eat strategy for breakfast, and politics may be the knife and fork—but we, as leaders, are the ones setting the table. Strive to be the leader who brings the good coffee, keeps the drama to a minimum, and creates an environment where people can thrive. And if all else fails, just remember: even the toughest lessons make for great stories later. (And maybe a therapy session or two.)

Here's to leading with integrity, laughing at the chaos, and never, ever becoming The Fool. Cheers!

ABOUT THE AUTHOR

Dallan Elk

Dallan Elk currently works with Zaxby's after spending most of his career with brands like Disney, Universal, Six Flags, and others. Hailing from the deep south, South Africa, he was educated at the University of Georgia.

His passions are his family (a lovely wife, 2 children, a dog, 5 birds) and his avid collection of tequila. While the tacos are a close second, his favorite Zaxby's meal is a spicy signature sandwich, extra seasoned fries, with 90% Diet Coke/10% lemonade to drink.

When We Lead Differently: The Quest for Respected Leadership

Danira Ibarra Beckmann

The Call to Leadership

Every great leader's journey begins with a defining moment—an internal call to adventure. Mine came in the form of a quiet promise, born out of shame and vulnerability, as I stood before my younger cousins, unable to read in English. It was then that I swore to myself: I would learn. I would rise. I would lead.

My first trial came on my first day at an American school when my third-grade science teacher called on me to read aloud. The words blurred, my voice faltered, and the sting of embarrassment was nearly unbearable. But instead of allowing the moment to defeat me, I turned it into a fuel source. I dedicated myself to mastering the language, knowing that resilience, determination, and perseverance would shape not only my ability to read—but my ability to lead.

The lesson was clear: The path to leadership is paved with challenges, and every challenge is an opportunity to grow stronger.

The Trial of Adversity

The second stage of any hero's journey is the trial of adversity. As I began my professional path, it took unexpected turns. At one point, I found myself unemployed—a seeming setback that instead became a gift, allowing me to spend time with my infant child. But soon, the call of purpose beckoned me once again.

I accepted a role as a membership coordinator at a nonprofit. Excited to make a difference, I worked tirelessly to expand our outreach. Yet, I soon faced a major obstacle: my supervisor, though well-meaning, was not a leader. She lacked vision, mentorship, and the ability to inspire her team.

Despite the lack of guidance, I pressed on, proposing creative strategies, only to have my contributions overlooked or credited elsewhere. A defining moment came when I presented a plan to build partnerships. Rather than encouragement, I received reprimands. My enthusiasm waned, and soon, I recognized that I had lost sight of my own leadership values. I had allowed the environment to define me instead of shaping the environment itself.

Realizing that the work environment was stifling my growth, I faced a difficult but necessary decision. I apologized to my supervisor, not for my beliefs or efforts, but as a final gesture of professionalism. Internally, however, I knew I was done fighting an uphill battle. The spark that once fueled my ambition had dimmed. The excitement I once felt in tackling challenges had been replaced by quiet resignation. I no longer pushed boundaries, questioned inefficiencies, or sought to innovate—I simply went through the motions.

Somewhere along the way, I had allowed my role to become just a job, something I had once sworn I would never accept. The realization was sobering. I had always believed in finding purpose in my work, in striving for environments that encouraged growth, creativity, and impact. But now, I was stuck in a cycle of complacency, a version of myself I didn't recognize. Deep down, I knew that staying meant compromising not only my ambitions but also my integrity.

Ultimately, I understood that growth sometimes requires walking away. Staying would have been the easier choice, but easy was not what I had set out to pursue. And so, with a heavy heart but a clear mind, I made the decision: it was time to move on.

The lesson: A leader does not simply exist within an organization—they shape it. When faced with an environment that stifles growth, a true leader must make a choice: fight to transform it or find a new battlefield where their leadership can thrive.

The Path of Wisdom

Through this experience, I discovered three fundamental truths about leadership:

1. **Seek Organizations with Growth Potential**—A leader must choose a setting that fosters development, encourages learning, and provides clear paths for advancement.
2. **Value Leadership Experience**—A strong leader is both a student and a mentor. Without effective leadership above us, we stagnate.
3. **Engage with Purpose**—A true leader does not simply work for a paycheck but pushes boundaries, challenges norms, and leaves an impact.

These lessons now shape the way I approach my career. They remind me to remain intentional in my professional choices, to seek out environments that foster leadership and innovation, and to never lose sight of the bigger picture—personal and collective growth.

The Mastery of Influence, Culture, and Purpose

As I studied leadership—both formally in college and through my professional experiences—I realized a simple truth: leadership is about impact, not authority.

Titles can be given, but respect is earned through vision, influence, and the ability to inspire. A leader's environment can uplift or undermine. I've worked under visionary leaders, but I've also seen leadership used as a weapon, breeding fear instead of innovation.

Ironically, one of the most impactful figures in my journey led through fear and intimidation. They didn't inspire me—they showed me exactly the kind of leader I never wanted to be.

Every interaction with this manager felt like a test I was meant to fail. In one-on-ones, they didn't strengthen my ideas—they dismantled them. Proposals were met with doubt, risks were inflated, and any autonomy came with an unspoken warning: "If you fail, you're on your own."

I dreaded those weekly meetings—they slowly chipped away at my confidence. Over time, I began second-guessing every decision. Progress stalled, and my work suffered—not from lack of ability, but from an environment that drained my courage to lead boldly.

Looking back, I realize the problem wasn't just one person—it was the culture of the organization. There was no room for mistakes, no space to grow. The unspoken rule was survival over innovation. That experience taught me a lasting lesson: leadership isn't just about the individual—it's about the environment they shape and the values their organization upholds.

Earlier in my career, I chased salary and titles, assuming upward mobility meant success. But I've since learned to look beyond the paycheck and carefully assess company culture. Now, before accepting any opportunity, I ask:

- Do employees genuinely live the company's values, and are leaders held to them?
- Does the environment encourage growth, prioritize learning, and treat mistakes as opportunities?

I now seek workplaces where leadership means empowerment and growth. To me, true leadership isn't about authority—it's about impact. And the kind of impact we choose to make is what truly defines us.

The takeaway: leadership isn't just about personal success—it's about the environment we create. A leader's greatest responsibility is to foster a culture where people feel safe to innovate, take risks, and grow.

The Power of Mentorship

Every hero has a mentor—someone who offers wisdom and steadiness through uncertainty. For me, that mentor reshaped my understanding of leadership, showing me it's not about personal achievements, but about empowering others to succeed.

Early in my leadership roles, I believed strength meant having all the answers, pushing relentlessly, and delivering results at all costs. But I soon learned that real leadership is about lifting others as you climb.

When I was tasked with building a Program Management Office (PMO), I realized success depended not just on my skills, but on the team. It was my first time leading nine people, and given past experiences with difficult managers, I was determined to do things differently.

The team had potential, but also gaps. Some had strong technical skills but lacked curiosity; others aligned with our strategic goals but needed support to grow. I invested time to understand each person's strengths, challenges, and aspirations. As I learned more about them, the PMO began to take shape.

Over the next three years, we laid the groundwork—defining roles, creating growth opportunities, and establishing policies. But beyond operations, I knew success hinged on something deeper: trust. Every element was refined, questioned, and improved. But the PMO would only thrive if the team believed in its vision and saw how it could shape their own careers.

Leading wasn't always easy. There were sleepless nights, replaying tough conversations with team members feeling overwhelmed or uncertain. I often joked that leadership was harder than parenting a teenager.

The lesson: leadership isn't a solo journey. A leader's greatest achievement is not their own success—but the success of those they guide.

The Final Test—Balancing Empathy + Accountability

One of leadership's greatest challenges is knowing when to push and when to step back. I once managed an employee who resisted feedback, avoided accountability, and showed little interest in growth. At first, I took it personally, believing I had failed as a leader. But my mentor offered a crucial insight: *not everyone chooses to grow.*

I had already learned to prioritize my team's needs—but I came to understand that competency matters just as much. Balancing both required regular check-ins, honest conversations, and a deep commitment to each person's development.

Through this, I discovered a powerful truth: when my team shines, I shine too. Their growth and well-being must come before my own goals. That means advocating for their needs, providing resources, and valuing them not just as employees, but as individuals. Investing in people offers far greater rewards than any personal milestone.

But this kind of leadership didn't come easily. I remember a time when I was frustrated with an underperforming employee. Missed deadlines and slipping productivity consumed my attention. I was ready to act—until my mentor offered a simple prompt: *"Pause and ask, what else might be going on?"*

I listened, and what I heard changed everything. The employee was dealing with personal challenges that were deeply affecting their work. That moment reshaped not just how I saw people—but how I saw leadership.

Empathy doesn't excuse poor performance; it seeks to understand its cause. Leaders who listen build trust, loyalty, and a culture where asking for help is safe. I also learned to tell the difference between those struggling but open to growth—and those who simply refuse.

The lesson: Invest in those who choose to grow—and know when to step away from those who don't.

Balancing Vulnerability + Professionalism in Leadership

While empathy is essential, boundaries are just as critical. Early in my leadership journey, I tried to be everything to everyone—saying yes to every request, sacrificing my well-being, and blurring the lines between personal and professional roles. I thought constant accessibility made me a better leader. In truth, I was stretching myself too thin, and it wasn't sustainable.

One of the hardest parts of leadership is balancing openness with professionalism. Vulnerability builds trust, but without clear boundaries, it can undermine a leader's role. Too distant, and you seem unapproachable. Too familiar, and you risk losing authority. Neither extreme works.

This delicate balance creates space for honest, sometimes tough conversations, while still reinforcing the leader's responsibility to guide and make difficult decisions. *A leader cannot be seen as just another friend.* There will be times when unpopular decisions are necessary for the team's success.

The challenge is that this balance isn't one-size-fits-all. Each team member is different, and no single leadership style fits everyone. I wanted strong relationships with my team—but I also needed to maintain their respect. Over time, I learned that boundaries don't create distance—they preserve effectiveness. *A leader who burns out trying to please everyone cannot inspire, guide, or support others.*

To lead well, I had to set clear expectations, stay professional, and show that authority and approachability can coexist. *True leadership isn't about being liked—it's about being trusted.* And trust is built through consistency, fairness, and respect.

Recognizing when to invest in someone—and when to step back—isn't just people management. It's strategic leadership. Sometimes the right move isn't to push harder—it's to let go. If someone refuses to take ownership, they must also accept the consequences.

Lesson Learned: Growth can't be forced—it's a choice. Leadership means helping people grow, and recognizing when they choose not to.

Leading by Example: The Foundation of Trust + Accountability

One of the most essential qualities of a strong leader is the ability to lead by example. This demands self-awareness, integrity, consistency, and emotional intelligence. In my experience, it's the most valued leadership style—because it requires both self-discipline and vulnerability. Leaders must embody the behaviors they expect from their teams, especially in challenging moments.

As a program manager, I set the benchmark for policies, procedures, and performance—not just for my team, but for myself. If I want my team to demonstrate accountability, commitment, and professionalism, I must model those qualities first. When leaders hold themselves to the same standards they set for others, they foster mutual respect and a culture of excellence.

But I've also learned that actions alone aren't always enough. Leadership isn't just about doing the right things—it's about helping others understand *why* they matter. Explaining the reasoning behind decisions, policies, and expectations builds clarity and trust. Transparency can be the difference between reluctant compliance and genuine buy-in.

Leading by example sounds simple—but it's far from easy. It requires unwavering consistency. Anyone can lead well when conditions are ideal, but true leadership is tested during times of stress and uncertainty. When a leader remains calm, focused, and solution-oriented, the team is more likely to do the same. When a leader panics, the ripple effect is immediate.

Leading by example also takes patience. Trust and credibility don't form overnight. Leaders earn respect over time by consistently demonstrating integrity, accountability, and a strong work ethic. But, once trust is broken, it's difficult to rebuild. That's why leadership isn't just about making the right choices—it's about making them consistently, even when no one's watching.

This is why consistency matters. Trust isn't built in a single moment—it's reinforced through steady, reliable action. Leadership is a long-term investment in people, and leading by example is the surest way to create a culture of accountability and excellence.

The Journey's End—and the Legacy That Follows

Every quest must come to an end, but the impact of a great leader extends far beyond their own journey. Leadership isn't about titles, status, or power—it's about influence, trust, and the ability to bring out the best in others. True leaders don't measure success by personal accolades, but by the growth of those they guide. Their legacy isn't written in achievements alone, but in the lives they've shaped and the confidence they've inspired.

As I continue my journey, I no longer chase promotions or prestige. Instead, I seek opportunities to mentor, to create environments where growth is nurtured, and to empower others to lead with integrity and purpose. Leadership isn't about standing above others—it's about standing beside them, lifting them up, and giving them the tools and belief to thrive.

The true measure of leadership lies not in what we accomplish alone, but in the legacy we leave through those we uplift.

The final lesson is this: Leadership isn't defined by the road we walk—it's defined by the paths we clear for others. It's about planting seeds of wisdom, resilience, and vision, knowing that the greatest impact may be one we never fully see.

And so, the quest continues—not for personal gain, but for the leaders yet to rise.

ABOUT THE AUTHOR

Danira Beckmann

Danira is the Innovation + Technology Program Manager for the City of Savannah. She is passionate about innovation and the strategic execution of transformational projects. In her first five years at the City of Savannah, she established the city's inaugural program management office, introducing its first project management methodology. This methodology has played a crucial role in the successful delivery of over twenty transformational initiatives, fostering a reputation for accountability and ensuring that projects deliver on their objectives.

Danira is driven by a passion for innovation and the strategic execution of transformational projects. With a proven ability to lead cross-functional collaborations and implement impactful solutions, she is committed to enhancing organizational efficiency and fostering a culture of accountability and continuous improvement.

Recognized for her drive, thoroughness, and strong work ethic, Danira exemplifies accountability and expects her teams to uphold the same standards in their performance.

When not working, Danira enjoys watching her boys play soccer and spending time with her family in Savannah, GA. Her guiding belief: Leadership isn't about personal success—it's about empowering others, clearing paths for their growth, and leaving a legacy through those we inspire to lead with purpose and integrity.

When Being Right Isn't Enough

Christine Coz

Two of my favorite sayings are: *Adults are just varnished children in a bigger, more dangerous sandbox,* and *We're all the walking wounded.* Have I succeeded in getting your attention, or are you ready to turn the page? If you're of the latter group, please bear with me. I can't promise that it will get better, but hopefully, my reasoning will make staying worth your while.

Each of us sees the world through a unique frame of reference, shaped by our experiences, early relationships, perceptions, and the filters we've developed over time. This lens influences everything: how we interpret the world, build friendships, form opinions, and navigate professional relationships. I'd like to share a few lessons learned through my own lens, shaped by my years in the sandbox and the layers of protective varnish I've gathered over time.

Before I get into the hand-wringing retrospective and my best attempt at lessons learned, I'd like to tell you a little bit about myself.

I was always an over-achiever. By the time I entered kindergarten, I already knew how to do long division and multiplication, thanks to a mother who loved math. So when the teacher made us finger paint, I went home dejected, disappointed, and wholly unimpressed! (Feel free to laugh; I certainly do now.) At the time, though, I told my mother that I was not overly pleased with my experiences at school.

A few years later, I skipped a grade and frustrated the principal when I was still bored. I don't share this to give myself a pat on the back, but to set the scene. This is the thread that has run through much of my life and career: always seeking more, always pushing forward, and rarely satisfied with the status quo.

As a girl who loved math and science, I was sure I'd pursue a career in a related field. But, when I finished grade 13 (yes, back when that extra year was still a thing and mandatory for university prep), I found myself wanting to be a journalist. At the time, there were two standout journalism schools, one in my hometown, a large metropolitan city, and one in the nation's capital.

As a first-generation North American, my parents weren't keen on the idea of me leaving town for school. Since I wasn't allowed to attend my top choice, I pivoted. Looking back, I sometimes wonder about that leap from math and science to journalism. But in truth, it wasn't a leap at all. It was still me. The same curious mind, obsessed with truth, facts, and uncovering the root cause of any issue.

In the end, I chose to study economics. At the time my backup plan was accounting. It made good use of my math skills and had come easily to me in high school. By age 14, I had already taken an adult bookkeeping course at night school and spent my high school years doing part-time bookkeeping for small businesses, working alongside an accounting firm. My university classes were mostly math and economics, where women made up maybe 10% of the cohort.

In third year, a science course introduced me to SAS, a programming language used for statistical analysis. I also took a third-generation programming language course in PASCAL. I found computers fascinating, and that curiosity sparked a shift in direction.

By now, you probably have a pretty clear picture of me: curious, competitive, quiet but strong-minded and strong-willed, and admittedly somewhat impatient. I've always set a high bar for myself, and importantly, I set it just as high for everyone else. As a woman, I believed that I had to outperform the men around me to succeed; a belief enforced by my mother. I love her to bits, but she shared many of these same traits and often told me, "Women can outshine men—we just have to be better than them!

I've gathered more lessons and themes from my career than could ever fit into one chapter. Truthfully, I could fill several books. In some ways, I was ahead of the curve. Today's gig economy normalizes moving from job to job, but 30+ years ago, most people stayed with an organization until they retired or were pushed out. Not me. I was never a political animal, and boredom or too much internal politics was reason enough to move on. Typically, around year five, I often found it was time for a change. Industry vertical didn't matter. Public or private, it was always energizing to dig into the inner workings of a new business model. I honestly believe I learned and earned more by switching things up. Over time, I also realized that consensus-driven decision-making cultures moved too slowly for my liking. I preferred working with people who were willing to stick their necks out and push for the right things to be done, and done with urgency.

Lesson 1: Change can be invigorating and educational

Just make the change with intention, and for the right reasons.

If you haven't already embraced this new world, know that long-term employment with a single organization is increasingly rare, and sometimes less desirable. Your best strategy? Get comfortable with change. Build resilience by arming yourself with in-demand skills: strong self-awareness (yes, self-talk counts), excellent communication, curiosity, and a desire to understand the business and not just the tech.

Early on, I realized that to be truly effective in IT, you had to understand the business almost as well as the non-IT folks. That's how you earn their trust, decode what they're asking for, and deliver meaningful solutions. I was fortunate to be an early adopter of fourth-generation programming languages, which led me to Rapid Application Development (RAD). I used quick visual prototypes to show end-users how I interpreted their requests. This bridged the gap between ideas and execution.

Over time, I became deeply knowledgeable about several industries—health care, pensions, banking, aerospace—and earned formal accreditations in many of them. That ego I mentioned earlier often whispered, *If they can learn it, so can I.* Today, I'd revise that to: *So must you.* IT is no longer just an enabler, it's embedded in the business fabric. Or at least, it should be viewed as such.

Speak the language of the business. Understand its pressures and strategic goals. That's how you move from being seen as a support function to being recognized as a partner in delivering outcomes.

Consider conducting an annual SWOT (strengths and weaknesses) analysis of your IT team and pairing it with an environmental PESTLE scan of your sector. Share both with your team. Help them see not only how the business is evolving but how they can grow to meet its needs. Change isn't coming—it's already here. Make sure your team is ready.

Lesson 2: It's OK

It's okay to ask questions, to ask for help, and to not be the best at everything on the team. That may seem obvious, but early in my IT career, these were things I really struggled with. The fear of not knowing everything, or not being the best, shaped much of my formative years. I was also quite shy, and that made things even harder. Let's face it: no one can be the best at everything, and yet anything less—failure—is something we're rarely taught to accept, let alone embrace.

I started my career in the aerospace industry. As a young, female, non-engineer in a very male-dominated, technical environment, showing vulnerability simply wasn't an option. I remember one particularly grueling weekend: from Friday night through Sunday at 10 p.m., I was holed up in the data center completing a long-overdue upgrade of a critical cluster of machines and all the layered software. The upgrade had been delayed for two years due to a Department of Defense configuration lockdown, so it was no small task.

When I walked into our 9 a.m. Monday status meeting, completely exhausted, my new boss—an engineering-scientist—looked at me and said flatly, "I didn't think you could do it." That was his response after

I had worked nearly 48 straight hours. He had assumed I would call him for help at some point, and when I didn't, instead of viewing it as a sign of capability, he saw me as a threat. I was young. I was female. I didn't have an engineering degree. And just before he took over as my manager, I'd been given a distinguished performance award. His response? "I didn't get one, and I was part of the team that delivered the Space Arm!"

Needless to say, I was no longer in his good graces.

That mindset worked in reverse, too. I remember being asked to set up an X.400 mail gateway to Johnson Space Center. These were the early days of networked communication—hopping through ARPA-NET-like systems, layered protocols, and clunky directory services. The company brought in a consultant to help with the task, but after a few days of him quietly reading manuals, I asked my boss to let me handle it alone. The challenge was too interesting to pass up, and true to form, I put a heavy load on myself.

In hindsight, I should've used the opportunity to learn in tandem with the consultant. It would've reduced the pressure, led to a more sustainable solution, and frankly, I should've cut him some slack—this was niche, complex tech. But that just wasn't my nature at the time.

As I moved into leadership, I came to deeply value team members who were comfortable asking for help. It's incredibly difficult to support someone who won't admit they're struggling. I discovered that my sweet spot was and still is teaching. That lingering fear of asking for help still pops up in some areas of my life, but my passion for helping others succeed has helped me confront it. Teaching forced me to embrace vulnerability, and taught me how powerful it can be when we use it to lift others.

Lesson 3: Find a mentor, ask questions and listen!

In keeping with the theme so far, I also didn't fully appreciate the value of having mentors, or even just *a* mentor. Looking back, it's clear that having one can be a tremendous career boost, and it's certainly not a sign of weakness (here we go again).

The closest I came was during my nine years at a pension company, where the CEO became something of a mentor figure. She gave me my first management role, but smartly started me off in an acting assignment before making it permanent. As she put it, and I'm paraphrasing, "Christine, you're moving from a technical role where you could be right 90+% of the time to a management role where you'll be right or prepared maybe 60% of the time. Management is full of judgment calls, and that's not an easy transition."

She was absolutely right. You can make the leap into leadership, but the nuances of managing both up and down take time and experience to master. I didn't lean on her wisdom as much as I should have, and I definitely could've saved myself a few hard lessons. Having someone who's already navigated the politics, stakeholders, and tough career decisions is an amazing gift.

And mentoring works both ways. I've always looked for opportunities to give back, especially through university co-op programs. Sharing lessons learned with students—what went right, but more importantly, what didn't—felt both useful and rewarding.

I even brought that spirit home. At dinner, I'd tell my kids stories from my day: the missteps, the recoveries, and what I might do differently next time. Thankfully, they listened.

Lesson 4: Let people really get to know who you are, vulnerabilities and all (but carefully)

As you move through your career, whether managing up or down, I've come to deeply appreciate the value of transparency and approachability. And let me tell you, that takes finesse. Learning to show who you are, sharing your passion without coming on too strong or too passive, and reading the room effectively is a skill that develops over time.

Focusing on competence alone, e.g.,"I got it done, didn't I?" simply isn't enough. If people feel comfortable with your intentions, they'll usually forgive a less-than-perfect delivery. But if they feel threatened or unsure of your motivations, even routine conversations can be over-analyzed and misunderstood.

The key is balance: show compassion, humor, curiosity, and openness to other perspectives. Be patient. For me, allowing people to see past the surface took time—largely because I'd internalized the idea that strength meant self-containment. My strength was real, but it lived beneath a quiet, reserved demeanor. That duality sometimes made it hard for others to calibrate; when I *did* speak up strongly, it stood out more—especially if people didn't know me well or weren't used to hearing my voice in the room.

A sense of humor and willingness to listen, especially when confronted with personality types dramatically different from your own, can make all the difference. Even in high-stakes situations like presenting to the board, letting people see what motivates you and how that aligns with the organization's goals can build trust and give you room to lead.

One important caveat: vulnerability is not the same as weakness. Early in my management career, I led a unionized team. That wasn't inherently a problem, but I didn't fully understand the dynamics at play. I wanted to be accessible, approachable, even friendly...but I went too far. My openness was misinterpreted and even taken advantage of in some cases. That experience taught me that approachability and vulnerability must be paired with discernment. You can absolutely be human and authentic, but keep your eyes open while you do it.

Lesson 5: Your boss is human, go easy!

For me, nurturing and supporting staff always came naturally. But seeing *my* superiors as people who needed support? That took much longer to learn.

Early in my career, I assumed that anyone in a senior role had it all figured out. They'd already "made it," so surely they didn't need encouragement or support, right? Wrong. The higher you climb, the more the pressure builds, and it's coming from all sides: executive peers, demanding business goals, team expectations, and the ever-present undercurrent of organizational politics.

Leaders at the top may not always show it, but they need to surround themselves with people they can trust. People they can bounce ideas off, confide in, and know will have their back. That kind of relationship is rare and valuable—and it doesn't just happen. It takes time, trust, and a genuine willingness to understand their world.

You earn the right to speak your mind. And once you've earned it, use it wisely. Steering conversations and influencing decisions without overpowering them requires skill, timing, and an awareness of how your message is landing. Think about how your last message was received, and refine your approach until you get it right.

And don't forget the simple things: invite your boss for a coffee. Ask how *they're* doing. Show them that you see the person, not just the position. It might feel awkward at first, especially in today's remote or hybrid work environments, but make an effort to connect. That personal touch builds real trust, and trust builds influence.

Seems obvious now, but it took me longer than it should have to figure that one out.

Looking Back, Moving Forward

If the younger me had heard these lessons earlier in my career, I might have breathed a little easier. I would have carried less pressure, expected less perfection from myself and others, and shared more openly. These days, I spend far more time in self-reflection. I've come to realize that the journey itself is as valuable, if not more so, than achieving the next target. So why not make it enjoyable for yourself *and* the people around you?

I return to those early ideas that have stuck with me: adults in a sandbox, and the walking wounded. Becoming an adult, especially a *professional* adult, is often just layering new roles and expectations on top of the foundation laid in childhood. Were you the entertainer, always seeking attention? The people-pleaser? The one who didn't like to share? Those traits don't vanish; they just get polished over with layers of experience and habit. But that inner child is still in there, shaping how we show up at work and in life.

The phrase *walking wounded* is one I use often. Regardless of how easy or difficult your life has been, we all develop scabs in response to trauma, big or small. Those experiences shape how we respond to stress, feedback, risk, and relationships. For me, the work now is to embrace who I am, to bring the best version of myself into each situation consciously and deliberately, and to extend that same grace to others, knowing they're likely trying to do the same. *Hopefully*.

So, embrace your uniqueness—but don't use it as armor. If I could speak to my younger self, I'd be kind. I'd encourage creativity. I'd remind her that the play and imagination we so freely express in childhood deserve space in adulthood, too. They make the journey richer, more meaningful—and a lot more fun.

ABOUT THE AUTHOR

Christine Coz

Christine Coz is an Executive Counselor for CIOs, CISOs and other IT Executives at InfoTech Research Group. Prior to joining InfoTech she was a CIO ad CISO most recently in the healthcare sector and is known for operational transformation of IT.

In her most recent role, Christine led the consolidation of two of the world's largest healthcare diagnostic repositories which had direct impact on access to medical diagnostic results facilitating healthcare for millions of patients and involved hundreds of hospitals and private clinics.

She also led the technology merger of two government crown corporations, Ontario Realty Corporation and Infrastructure Ontario rationalizing the application and infrastructure portfolios, while consolidating the operational teams.

She has been a cybersecurity leader for the past 30 years and has initiatives and grown security practices both in public and private industry.

Christine is passionate about driving operational excellence and technological advancement where it serves to improve effective and efficient service delivery. She is a change agent! She thrives on opportunities to enhance the operation and service delivery model with a focus on customer support. Productivity, effectiveness, and efficiency are her goal!

Her motto of "bake it in" has been a staple for years as she believes that processes need to be integrated and baked in by design. Too much time and effort is spent trying to retrofit quality, security, risk containment far too late in the process.

Outside of work Chris love to garden, cook, travel and spend time with family and friends.

When Defining You-nique Success

Charles O. Beierle

Choosing a Right Answer

Imagine a room full of people—the last conference or class session you attended. Now picture the speaker, someone you know only from announcements and a brief introduction, posing this question: *"Do you think I am a successful person?"* Then, they follow up with, *"Are you a successful person?"*

How quickly could you answer the first question? And what about the second?

If you like line graphs, you might picture success as a straight line, climbing steadily toward the top right—where time is the X-axis and success, usually measured in material wealth, is the Y.

If you're a football fan, you might see success as a more jagged but still forward-moving path, a series of strategic plays progressing toward the goal.

Zoom out far enough, and the trajectory of any successful person's journey might look simple and straightforward. But in reality, that kind of simplicity is rare.

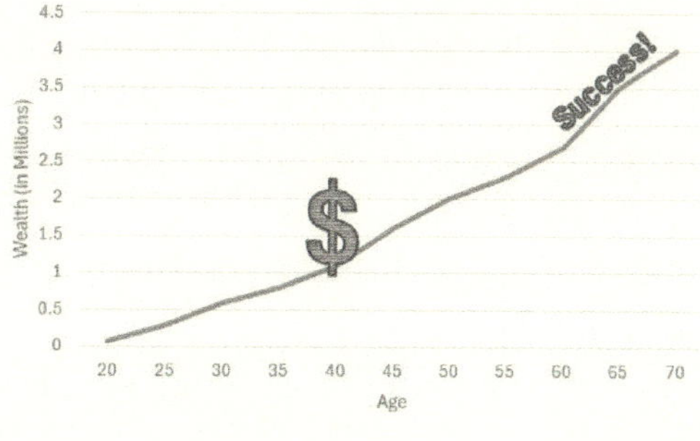

I suggest approaching this content the way an artist mixes paint. Each reader will take different elements of what I offer, blending them into their own thinking. There's no wrong way—except the one that leads to *"I can't do anything about my success."* Whatever color that paint is, avoid it.

In this text, I offer a light framework for success, along with a brief story of someone I consider successful, to illustrate the key concepts.

The majority of this work comes from presentations I've shared with student and young professional groups as part of career development engagements. It's a passion of mine and a key part of my own success plan.

More than anything, I hope that one day, someone who has heard me speak or read these words will find their own version of success—and that, in some small way, I'll have played a part in it.

A Framework—Dream, Plan, Execute, Review, Repeat

Dream! Dreams are the big picture—expansive, durable, and resilient to all but the most drastic life events, as long as we let them be. It's important to remember that dreams can evolve, shaped by experience, perspective, and maturity.

That's why you shouldn't treat dreams like goals. Goals serve as the support beams of a dream, the poles holding up the tent—but unlike dreams, goals come with structure and rigidity.

Let's try a quick exercise. Feel free to change the character as you see fit.

Imagine you dream of being an astronaut. What does that look like in your mind? Do you see yourself gazing back at Earth, rocketing into orbit, or even standing on the surface of Mars?

Now, shift your thinking. Instead of dreaming of being an astronaut, imagine your goal is to become one. What does that mental image look like now? Is it a list of milestones? A step-by-step plan to qualify, train, and compete for a place among the chosen few?

You're going to need a plan. And one of the most important things to understand is that *your plan must be yours.* The steps, timelines, tools, and people involved should be tailored to fit *you*—as structured or flexible as necessary to keep you moving forward.

Sound familiar? You've probably heard something similar in the context of fitness plans or diet changes. It's fundamental advice—not groundbreaking, but essential. Success requires the right balance of discipline, motivation, and drive, but how you mix those elements is entirely up to you.

Your plan is what turns dreams into reality. And because reality is unpredictable, your plans will need to evolve. Change is inevitable—*adaptability is key.*

We can't ignore the elephant in the room, which is history. If we skipped over it, this entire discussion would be pointless. After all, we're talking about our own version and measure of success, not a guarantee of the impossible.

Your past and your current resources are facts—they define your starting point. And conveniently, that starting point is always *right now.* To build a real, actionable plan, you must be honest about where you've been and what you have at your disposal. That also means owning your future missteps without over-blaming the past.

If you're looking for an escape clause, you might want to check with the Department of Failure Assurance—though I hear their "Limited Liability for Future Damages" policy is pretty restrictive.

Planned pauses are still part of the plan. Life rarely unfolds in a neat, linear sequence—our dreams and the plans that support them will inevitably have starts and stops. Some will catch us off guard, but many are necessary to keep things moving forward.

So, expect, accept, and plan for pauses.

But here's a word of caution: *pausing is not the same as procrastinating.* A pause is an intentional break, built into your plan to ensure the timing is right. Putting something off, on the other hand, is just delaying progress without any real benefit. Know the difference, and avoid the latter.

Career trajectory is a great example of planning in action. When mapping out your path, do you take the time to build experiences that foster resilience—enhancing your ability to empathize with those you may one day lead? What is that worth?

Or, do you take the "burn rubber" approach, racing up the corporate ladder as quickly as possible because your plan prioritizes the perceived status or benefits of a particular title? Either path requires careful planning, but with different trade-offs.

Now, what happens if you take the fast-track route and suddenly realize you're the only person at your level without a key qualification—maybe a certain degree or hands-on experience with an important client segment? Did you skip that step because it made you uncomfortable? And if you did, can you really blame those who promoted you for the gap? Does pointing fingers solve the problem?

Be sure to plan pauses that allow things to develop and mature with long-term success in mind. It would be irresponsible not to address a key aspect of next steps: pausing and planning. As you progress in certain career paths—technology management, for example—there are fewer positions available, and only a fraction of those are open at any given time. That's why part of your plan should include a "ready to jump" check. This is the moment when you'll be poised to seize an opportunity when it arises.

Don't forget to factor in your professional brand and visibility during pauses. Connections are invaluable for career progression.

Communicate your plan to those you trust and those whose participation is necessary. Be open to feedback and adjust your plan as needed, even if those changes make things more challenging. Ignore the sugar-coating and unhelpful suggestions—focus on creating a plan that you are truly motivated to pursue. If you find that a key ally or resource will no longer be available, don't hesitate to redraw your plan.

Execution is where it all comes together. With your dreams clearly defined, the necessary resources in place, and the right support lined up, it's time to take action.

Review your progress. Assess your approach, resources, and commitment. Do you feel successful yet? Why or why not? At this point, you might realize that you haven't defined specific goals or metrics to measure success. Don't worry—there are plenty of books, blogs, and YouTube videos to help with goal-setting and metrics. The goal of this chapter is simply to get comfortable with what you want in terms of goals and metrics, rather than focusing on the exact measures themselves.

For your accountability homework, perform a damage assessment. What were the unintended consequences of your plan? Did it harm any relationships or impact your credibility? As part of your review and future planning, take time to consider these aspects and plan how to address them. Ask for feedback, offer apologies, or admit when you were wrong—then take steps to improve.

I recommend you assess your progress and any potential "damage" on a daily basis. View shortcomings as opportunities to do better tomorrow, and see that as a positive part of the process.

Easy, right? Well, whether you were successful this time or not, we're not finished yet. Go back to that dream paragraph and start again. Rinse and repeat—find your success at your pace, on your terms.

Expect the unexpected. Mistakes and bad luck will find you sooner or later, but as the venerable Jerry Jeff Walker said, "every drop of water shapes the stone." If we are fortunate enough to have time, we must use it wisely. I've heard it said that the wisest people are those who have lived long enough to make mistakes—and learn from them.

With a basic framework in place for pursuing success, let's shift to a story. Examining what success looks like in practice will help us refine our own definitions and understand how successful people operate. That clarity will make the framework even more powerful.

My Successful Person

I believe we build our definition of success from environmental feedback—observing what actions (or inactions) lead to outcomes we judge as favorable, whether for ourselves or others. But here's the key question: how do we determine what is truly favorable?

Tired of all the questions? Fair enough. We'll shift to story time. But keep in mind—this chapter isn't about prescribing the formula for success. There's no magic diet pill.

For me, the "great plan" was simple: go to college, land a wonderful job, get married, start a family. A management position by age 25, and—get this—retirement by 45. Later, I adjusted that last part to authoring a book by 45 instead.

Well, here I am, co-writing a book at age 45. I also just earned a master's degree, opening doors to potentially teaching college-level technology business courses—either alongside or instead of learning how to build tiny houses someday.

So there you have it—my past and present goals and dreams. But this story isn't about me. I'm not here to dwell on my own journey because this is really about you.

The success bar was set high from the start.

My grandfather stands out as a classic example of a traditionally successful person. Born into a large family in San Antonio, TX, he grew up during the Great Depression—a time when survival often depended on sheer grit. As a child, he sold newspapers on street corners to help support his family.

When World War II broke out, he joined the U.S. Navy, but his service was cut short after a particularly unfortunate incident—a ship hatch came loose and struck him in the head, ending his time in uniform.

After leaving the Navy, he tried college but eventually chose a different path. In the mid-1950s, he founded the family business—a move that, in many ways, defined his legacy. A familiar story for his generation.

He served as a member of the Texas House of Representatives, a role he took immense pride in. He was also active in the Chamber of Commerce and numerous business organizations. No matter where we went, someone would always stop to talk to Mr. Vallance—and that was another thing: no one called him by his first name except my grandmother. He was Grandfather to us and to everyone else, he was always Mr. Vallance.

Maybe it was his upbringing, but my grandfather never took out loans or used credit cards—at least, not that I remember, and we talked a lot. Maybe he had a gas card, but otherwise, he paid for everything in cash. That was just who he was—he didn't owe anyone anything. He never seemed to worry about money, though he was certainly diligent about tracking where he spent it.

The family business was his major support vehicle for the various needs of the family, and like any family-run enterprise, it was both a blessing and at times a hardship. Many of our relatives lived within walking distance, so we grew up close. Since his passing, the family has spread out across the country, but in the ways that mattered most, my grandfather was undoubtedly successful.

Analysis

Now, let's break down the story to examine the actions and outcomes from different perspectives in search of a deeper understanding of how success is recognized and measured. I realize that many factors influence an individual's—or even an entire population's—perception of success. Consider my effort here as just one example, and apply your own thought process to stories you are familiar with.

Overcoming financial hardship is often seen as a measure of success. The Great Depression began in late 1929, when my grandfather was just 3 years old, and lasted through his teenage years as the country struggled to recover. During that time, unemployment soared to nearly 25 percent. For comparison, during the COVID-19 pandemic, the U.S. Bureau of Labor Statistics (BLS) reported that unemployment peaked at 14.7 percent in April 2020—the highest rate recorded since the BLS began tracking the data in 1948.

If surviving the Great Depression is considered a success, will future generations view those of us who endured the COVID-19 pandemic in the same way a hundred years from now? Think back to our earlier discussion about planning. Did you adapt your plans to account for the challenges of the pandemic, or did you treat it as a disruption to existing plans?

If simply surviving a serious economic crisis doesn't seem like a clear measure of success, what if I told you my grandfather was one of nine children? Does that change your perspective? Why or why not?

For some, the idea of growing up in a family that large is difficult to imagine. Providing for 11 people—even in good times—seems like an incredible challenge. On the other hand, if you come from a large family yourself or know someone who does, you might have a different perspective. Our personal experiences shape how we define success, influencing what we view as obstacles and what we consider achievements.

Discussing how we view earning money can be a sensitive topic, especially in my grandfather's case. He was just a child when he sold newspapers to help support his family. Some might see the difficult financial circumstances of the time as a mitigating factor, while others might view it as an early display of work ethic and resilience.

How do you see employment, hard work, and financial independence as attributes of success? It's worth examining the different facets of earning money, including subconscious factors we may not even realize. For example, was the work driven by a true necessity—such as avoiding hunger or homelessness—or was it simply part of a larger goal?

My own career has mostly consisted of office work in comfortable conditions, but early on, I spent time in the Texas heat, crawling through attics and tight spaces to run low-voltage cable for burglar alarms, video, and networking. I certainly earned less per drop of sweat in those days. If we were to compare two otherwise similar personal stories, would it be fair to judge one as more successful than the other based on the type of work involved?

How does this factor into your own planning? Are your choices driven by your personal definition of success, or do outside opinions influence what you pursue?

Military service and other forms of public service often influence how we define success. Do you see these commitments as markers of achievement? If so, is that belief something you've arrived at personally, or is it a perspective shaped by your environment?

There's no right or wrong answer here. The key is understanding where your values come from and why they resonate with you. It's not about changing your perspective—rather, it's about ensuring that the values you hold are truly your own and not just inherited assumptions.

Evaluating formal education as a measure of success is complex. In my grandfather's youth, fewer than 20 percent of people completed high school, and only about 14 percent had any college education. (CPS Historical Time Series Tables, 2024) According to the data, until the 1970s, females were more likely than males to finish high school. The gap began to close after World War II, something research has attributed to many returning soldiers struggling to find work and choosing to continue their education instead.

Of course, any discussion of educational attainment would be incomplete without acknowledging the significant racial disparities that have persisted over time. While gender differences in graduation rates followed a similar pattern across racial groups, the overall gap between white and non-white individuals has remained substantial throughout the historical data.

An individual's circumstances undeniably influence both access to education and the level of attainment. As with many criteria in assessing success, it's important to look beyond the surface. Education, while often a valuable tool, is not the sole determinant of a person's potential or accomplishments.

The last facet we will consider is how a person's actions—or inaction—toward their family shape our perception of their success. Of all the factors we've explored, this one often evokes the strongest, most polarized judgments, usually with the least amount of factual information to support them.

I recently read the comments section of a social media post criticizing a well-known actor for reposting her in-laws' GoFundMe campaign. The in-laws had lost everything in a devastating wildfire, and the fundraiser aimed to help them recover. Many people immediately condemned her, arguing that she should have simply replaced their possessions herself rather than asking others to contribute. But was she truly wrong? Did she already help privately? We don't know, do we?

Think about a time when you, or someone you know, faced a crisis. What's the first thing people usually ask? "What can I do?" In the community where I grew up—before the internet became what it is today—people responded to hardships in a more personal way. Fundraisers existed, but more often than not, people would ask for clothing sizes, favorite colors, or specific needs, then quietly collect and distribute items. Today, GoFundMe has largely taken over that role.

There's so much more we could unpack—grit, upbringing, finances, service, education, and family are just a few aspects of one person's story, shared here to illustrate the often-overlooked process of defining success. Hopefully, you now see how critical it is to explore this for yourself. Doing so fosters a deeper sense of fairness—not only toward others but also toward yourself.

Your Send Off

When I set out to share some ideas about success, I expected the effort to be complex and unique, but not as personal as it has turned out to be. It should be clear now, after going through this exercise and reflecting on your own stories, that these factors shape how we view ourselves, others, and how we interact with the world around us. Hopefully, you've also come to realize that our version of success is not set in stone—it should be determined by one person only… you. Take what you've learned here and apply it to your own life. Use it to consider the success of others, and especially when you inevitably find yourself helping someone else reflect on their future and what success means to them.

Bibliography

CPS Historical Time Series Tables. (2024, January 13). Retrieved from United States Census Bureau: https://www.census.gov/data/tables/time-series/demo/educational-attainment/cps-historical-time-series.html

U.S. Bureau of Labor Statistics. (13, May 2020). *The Economics Daily (TED).* Retrieved from U.S. Bureau of Labor Statistics: https://www.bls.gov/opub/ted/2020/unemployment-rate-rises-to-record-high-14-point-7-percent-in-april-2020.htm

ABOUT THE AUTHOR

Charles O. Beierle

Charles Beierle is a seasoned CIO in the financial services sector, renowned for his expertise in steering technology and cybersecurity initiatives during challenging times. He spearheaded a comprehensive effort to transition a large organization from full onsite operations to secure remote work during the COVID-19 pandemic. Additionally, he launched a responsible AI program within a heavily regulated industry and supported multiple legacy system transformations.

Charles is deeply committed to empowering future generations of technology-driven professionals who grasp the importance of risk management and self-investment. He strives to balance the adoption of cutting-edge technology with thoughtful decision-making. Charles possesses two remarkable skills: storytelling and problem-solving. The more complex the problem, the better the story!

In boardrooms, Charles is a favorite for his ability to make intricate technical content accessible to business leaders, regardless of their background. His motto, "Do Less Better," emphasizes a top-down commitment to excel in the most valuable tasks, contrasting sharply with the notion of "Do More with Less," which often implies increasing expectations despite limiting resources.

Charles mentors young individuals and adult career changers in technology and cybersecurity. He trains middle and high school students in cyber clubs, speaks at student conferences, and serves on college advisory boards. When he's not at work or teaching Charles is usually running miles on a trail somewhere in Texas.

When Fate Happens

Sallie Fulsom Wright

Lesson 1: Starting from the Bottom

Despite having no encouragement or guidance, I was fortunate enough to attend college. As a first-generation college student, I was expected to follow traditional roles for women. But the shifting cultural and political landscape opened up new possibilities.

Over the years, there's been plenty of discussion about inclusion, diversity, and equity. But classism? That was something I'd rarely heard mentioned—until I read *White Trash.* That book laid out in stark clarity what classism means and how deeply it has shaped, and continues to shape, the country.

As the youngest child of six, born to older parents who had already had their fair share of child rearing, my future seemed set: marry young, have babies, and barely scrape by in a tiny town in Oklahoma. But fate had other plans.

The U.S. was in the midst of a cultural revolution. The Vietnam War divided the nation. Hippies, free love, and bra burnings collided with protests for women's rights. It was the 1970s, and for the first time, women could open their own bank accounts, get credit cards—even own property. At 18, you were expected to stand on your own two feet, and my future was mine to decide.

During my senior year of high school, I received several academic scholarships—ones I hadn't even applied for. But with my limited exposure to the world, I had no clue what careers were out there. My oldest sister was a legal secretary, so I thought, *Well, why not?* I accepted a scholarship and went to college.

I started in the secretarial program and did well in every class but one. By the end of my first semester, I had transferred to the computer department—and that's where my real career began.

Lesson Learned: It's possible to break from limiting circumstances with determination and opportunity.

Lesson 2: First Job and Professional Struggles

As I neared the end of my coursework for an associate's degree, job interviews started coming my way. One opportunity stood out—a beginning computer programmer position at another university. I went in for my first interview and was offered the job on the spot.

With that, new challenges surfaced: Where would I live? What would I wear? How would I juggle finishing college while working full-time?

One of the biggest lessons I learned had to do with my boss—and his character.

When I started, my office didn't have a desk chair, so I was given a hard plastic one as a temporary fix. My boss made a big fuss about ordering me a proper chair, talking about it almost daily. After about eight weeks, it finally arrived. But instead of giving it to me, he decided he wanted it for himself. His old chair was then moved to my office.

That little stunt didn't go unnoticed—his actions made him look like a complete jerk. But it was an eye-opening experience for me. It taught me that how you treat people matters. The way he handled the situation made an impression, just not the one he intended.

Lesson Learned: I took on my first programming job while learning to balance work and school. Along the way, I also learned a valuable lesson: how you treat others shapes their perception of you. Respect matters.

Lesson 3: Rising to Leadership

Resilience and adaptability are key when starting a new role—especially under challenging circumstances.

After three years on the job, I had learned everything from operations to programming. I had built strong relationships with staff, faculty, and even some students. But I was getting bored, and with no clear path for advancement, I started looking for opportunities outside the university.

Then, at just 21, I was unexpectedly asked to apply for the CIO position after my direct supervisor left. That experience taught me more than just leadership—it showed me the unspoken rules of working in a male-dominated executive team.

I quickly realized that management bent the rules when it suited them. Policies weren't set in stone—they were adjusted as needed. I also learned that appearances mattered. If I wanted to be taken seriously, I had to dress extremely conservatively. And if I didn't want to be the one fetching coffee during meetings, I had to become a coffee drinker myself.

Surviving as the only woman in a room full of male executives meant constantly observing, adapting, and proving my worth. I had to be more prepared, more knowledgeable, and simply better at everything I did.

Lesson Learned: Thriving in a male-dominated environment requires resilience, adaptability, and the ability to navigate unspoken rules.

Lesson 4: Embracing Work Ethic and Growing Responsibilities

I worked long hours to modernize the IT organization, overhauling both hardware and software and transitioning from punch cards to terminals. I led a complete transformation of how college students enrolled in classes and received grades. I built a new data center, expanded and retooled the staff, and centralized computing to provide both administrative and academic solutions. Many of the principles I put in place decades ago still remain. I laid the foundation alongside a fantastic team of professionals.

It took me 10 years to earn my bachelor's degree, taking just one course per semester. But that slow pace turned out to be an advantage—I had a front-row seat to how students, faculty, and staff interacted with the very systems I helped build.

By all standards, I was too young for the level of authority I held. I was too young to do a lot of things, but I did them anyway. I learned that work ethic matters more than almost anything. I carried myself as if I were older, and most people believed it. I treated everyone with respect and delivered solutions on time.

I only fired one person during my time at the university. He didn't fit the culture—and he had no interest in working for a female boss. He dared me to fire him, so I did. It was a gut-wrenching experience, but it taught me to be much more thoughtful when hiring.

This role was full of firsts for me. My first leadership job. My first executive position. My first time hiring, firing, retooling, and modernizing an entire department. And it was just the beginning.

Lesson Learned: Work ethics and respect for others are paramount for success in leadership.

Other Learnings: **A Collection of Key Learnings:**

- **Choices have consequences:** For every decision, there is something you must give up.
- **Life isn't always fair:** Your unique qualities set you apart; embrace them.

- **Respect and kindness matter:** Treat everyone with kindness, no matter their circumstances.
- **Positive energy is essential:** People want to work with those who radiate positivity and respect.
- **Time is precious:** Use it wisely and limit exposure to negative influences.
- **Learn from every experience:** Whether successes or failures, all are opportunities for growth.
- **Work-life balance is key:** Don't let work overshadow the importance of family and personal life.
- **Adaptability is vital:** Embrace change and be open to learning new skills throughout life.

Lesson 5: Navigating Ageism in the Workforce

My first job laid the foundation for my career, positioning me for continued success, something for which I am deeply grateful. It wasn't planned; it was just fate. But looking back, I see another theme woven into my experience: ageism, especially when you're very young.

Today, I find myself at the other end of the spectrum. I've spent nearly 50 years in my field, and my passion for learning and making a difference has never faded. My journey has taken me from IT executive to executive counselor, coaching and guiding leaders across industries in the U.S. and beyond.

Ageism becomes glaringly obvious when only one-third of headhunters even consider candidates over 50. Silver hair isn't a mark of wisdom—it's a red flag. Wrinkles? A liability. Aging is one of the only forms of discrimination that remains socially acceptable, often treated as a punchline rather than a reality.

So, what do you do? You adapt. You tweak your résumé to omit anything older than 10-15 years. You remove graduation dates. You update your language—no more "programmers," only "developers." Some people dye their hair, get facelifts, and do whatever it takes to stay in the game.

In the C-suite, executive presence remains the deciding factor—but with a youthful undertone. I always tell my clients: dress just a little better than everyone else. Look polished. Look healthy. No beer bellies. No worn-out anything. Aging is inevitable, but not everyone gets the privilege of growing old.

Retirement, as we know it, was designed for a different era—when men were expected to live to 65 and retire at 60, enjoying five years before the "pearly gates." Today, if you make it to 60 or 65, you have an 85% chance of reaching 85. That means retirement can stretch 20-25 years. What then?

Without purpose, you wither. Retirement programs must evolve. Part-time work for older professionals needs to become the norm. Longer life spans mean longer careers, but getting hired past 50 requires strategy. How do you stay relevant? You keep moving. Keep learning. Stay fit. Maintain a positive outlook. Adapt to the future instead of clinging to the past.

Be the energy in the room. Focus on what people do right, not what they do wrong. Success is a choice. Misery won't get you anywhere. Not everyone is good or trustworthy—some will lie, take advantage, and even enjoy watching you fail. Learn from them. Then, rise above them.

Lesson Learned: Ageism is real, but experience, adaptability, and a strong sense of purpose can still create opportunities.

Wrapping it UP

When you start a new job, remember—you work *there* now. Stop referencing your old company. No one cares, and you'll only come across as someone who thinks they're better than everyone else. Celebrate your successes with your new team and your family, not your past.

Balance is everything. Your kids are only small once. You can sacrifice an entire weekend for work, only to be called in on Monday and told, *We love your work, but we're going in a different direction.* Don't let work take precedence over what truly matters.

Understanding the difference between *want* and *need* will transform how you prioritize. Have friends outside of work—because once you leave, most co-workers won't stay in touch, and soon enough, you'll forget their names. Workplace friendships are just that—co-workers who happen to like you.

ABOUT THE AUTHOR

Sallie Fulsom Wright

Sallie Fulsom Wright, BS, MA, CISSP, has 30+ years of experience in information technology executive leadership serving in the capacity of CIO, Associate Vice President and Chief Information Officer, Assistant Vice President and Deputy CIO, Assistant Vice Chancellor for Information Security and Chief Information Security Officer. She has worked for 4 tier-1 Research institutes including the University of North Carolina at Chapel Hill, the University of Alabama at Birmingham, Oklahoma State University and Georgia State University. She teaches computer science courses. Currently, she is teaching Cyber Security Classes for Emory University's partnership with the Georgia Women in Technology Program.

Sallie is currently a CIO & Executive Counselor for Info Tech Research Group working with CIOs, CISOs and other Executives to move their organizations to the next level of excellence. Prior to joining Info Tech, she spent 3 years as the CIO for Fulton County Government in Atlanta, Georgia focusing on digital transformation, modernization, strategic planning, and organizational redesign. She founded the CIO Regional Forum for collaborating within the government sector.

Ms. Wright was selected in 2018 as a top finalist in the InspireCIO Georgia CIO of the Year Award. In 2014 she was a top five finalist for the Technology Association of Georgia's (TAG) Diversity Leadership Awards. She was also a top five finalist for 2013 and 2014 TAG Excellence in Leadership Award. In August 2015, she was inducted into the PinkTech Hall of Fame. She is a speaker and moderator at local, regional, and national technology conferences. She serves as a mentor to students in the Georgia State University Robinson School of Business MBA program and other programs. She serves on the Georgia Public Defense Foundation Board, the Inspiredu Board, the Atlanta Technology Professionals Board, the SIM Atlanta Board, The Vendorship Board, Georgia Prosecutors Foundation and served for 10 years on the Technology Association of Georgia's Diversity, Equity, and Inclusion Board. Throughout the years she has taught Computer Science in various universities. She is a Certified Executive Coach and a Certified Leadership Coach.

Ms. Wright built information security organizations for Oklahoma State University, the University of North Carolina at Chapel Hill, and UAB. She worked for the Renaissance Computing Institute in the role of Director of Research Engagement where she participated in the development of multi-disciplinary grants for UNC Chapel Hill, Duke University, and North Carolina State University. She has led many enterprise projects for UAB including PCI Compliance and Web Presence. In addition, she co-founded the Southeast Region Higher Education Security Consortium. She was a founding member of the EDUCAUSE Higher Education Information Security Council for 10 years and served on the Southeast University Research Association (SURA), SANS Advisory Board and the CISO Executive Board.

Conclusion

As we draw the curtains on this remarkable journey through the careers of twenty distinguished information technology executives, we are left with an abundance of invaluable insights and practical knowledge. Each chapter has provided us with a window into the unique experiences and lessons learned by these industry leaders, showcasing the diverse paths and innovative tools that have shaped their professional trajectories.

The stories shared within these pages are more than mere anecdotes; they serve as a testament to the resilience, creativity, and adaptability required to thrive in the ever-evolving landscape of information technology. From the earliest days of their careers, navigating through uncharted territories, to the present where they lead with a vision for the future, these executives have demonstrated the power of continuous learning and the importance of embracing change.

One common thread that weaves through all their narratives is the significance of collaboration and mentorship. The value of building strong networks and fostering relationships cannot be overstated. Whether it was seeking guidance from seasoned experts or empowering the next generation of tech innovators, the role of human connection has been pivotal in their journeys.

Furthermore, the use of cutting-edge tools and technologies has been a cornerstone of their success. From leveraging data analytics to drive decision-making, to harnessing the capabilities of cloud computing and artificial intelligence, these executives have consistently embraced technological advancements to stay ahead of the curve.

Their experiences highlight the necessity of staying informed and agile in a field where innovation is relentless.

As we reflect on the collective wisdom imparted in this book, we are reminded that the road to success in information technology is not a solitary one. It is paved with the contributions of many, built on a foundation of shared knowledge and experiences. The lessons learned and tools utilized by these executives are now a part of our own toolkit, ready to be applied in our respective endeavors.

In conclusion, this compilation of insights serves as a beacon for aspiring IT professionals and seasoned experts alike. It underscores the importance of perseverance, adaptability, and the willingness to embrace new challenges. As we embark on our own journeys, let us carry forward the legacy of innovation and collaboration exemplified by these esteemed executives, and continue to push the boundaries of what is possible in the realm of information technology.

Made in the USA
Columbia, SC
28 April 2026

82454140R00132